Walt Disney

TREASURES

Walt Disney

TREASURES

Personal Art and Artifacts from The Walt Disney Family Museum

WALTER E. D. MILLER
And the Staff of The Walt Disney Family Museum

Foreword by Kirsten Komoroske

weldonowen

CONTENTS

PREFACE

I've always been deeply passionate about preserving and honoring the life and legacy of my grandfather, Walt Disney. He was an extremely curious man, and since his passing, the public maintains a fascination about his fabled legacy. Who was Walt Disney, and what made him so successful and talented at what he did? There are generations alive today who don't realize that he was a real person, and a very decent man—a man who worked hard all his life, who never gave up, who loved people, and who is much more than a corporate symbol, a brand name, or a title card at the beginning of your favorite film.

The interest in my grandfather—"Grampa" as we affectionally called him—never seems to wane. When I meet people and they learn that Walt Disney was my Grampa and I, his namesake—a big warm smile usually comes across their face, and the first thing they ask is: "Do you get into Disneyland for free?" Then they tell me how much *Bambi*, Mickey Mouse, or Disneyland meant to them growing up. People remember where they were on Sunday nights when he made his regular appearance on their television; they never forget crying during *Old Yeller* (1957); and they nostalgically reminisce the thrill of running down Main Street, U.S.A., to that first attraction of the day at the parks.

My older brother and sisters also have wonderful memories of staying overnight with Grampa Walt and Granny Lillian at their private Disneyland apartment, located above the Fire Station in Town Square. They would fall asleep to the distant animal roars of the *Jungle Cruise*'s soundscape and wake up early for a pre-dawn tour with Grampa. He was immeasurably proud of all his grandchildren—he wanted us to see and experience as much as possible and gain a whole different sensibility of what the park was all about.

I was only five years old when Grampa passed away, but I have great memories from a trip with Granny and Grampa and a few of my siblings down to San Diego for the day to visit SeaWorld. Although I don't recall snapping the only photograph I ever took of him, it's obvious Grampa was cooperating with the camera man and following the lens downward. Being so young and still unfamiliar with a camera, I was clearly taking the photo from far too low of an angle. He gradually bent down lower and lower, and the final picture is of him just about on his knees, with a little sandwich in one hand. It's such a great shot. This special photo is in the museum's collection and I treasure it to this day. Featured in this book is that photo on p. 40.

This memory is also particularly apt as filmmaking, art, and capturing stories has, in turn, become a passion in my life. My mother, Diane Disney Miller, and I helped establish the Walt Disney Family Foundation in 1995 and created the first iteration of The Walt Disney Family Museum: a virtual museum experienced by CD-ROM, which eventually evolved into a website. In continuing my passion for telling my grandfather's story, I also served as Executive Producer on documentary films such as *Walt: The Man Behind the Myth* (2001) and *Walt & El Grupo* (2008). The goal of these efforts was not only to expose broader audiences to the story of Walt Disney, but also to pay tribute to the many people who worked with him and helped bring his creative visions to life.

This work naturally evolved to working with my mother as she oversaw the design and construction of The Walt Disney Family Museum in San Francisco, California. During the early days of the museum project, it was envisioned as a place where we would conduct Foundation business while surrounded by an atmosphere that celebrated Walt and Lillian. The space would display our extensive collection of keepsakes and memorabilia, which had been stored in boxes and warehouses for far too long. The idea quickly flourished from merely showcasing our personal family items to creating something that the public could also enjoy, a place to experience the life story of Walt Disney, and we eagerly began locating and acquiring precious Disney artifacts from around the world. Eventually, our collection grew into a fully realized public nonprofit museum, with an overwhelming number of contributions from Walt's former colleagues, employees, and friends, in addition to other private donors and the historical collections housed at The Walt Disney Company.

My mother had considered several options for the location of the museum, but we learned that the Presidio of San Francisco, a former military base, was looking to lease out a number of its buildings. It quickly became the clear choice for the museum. The Presidio is the world's largest national park situated in an urban setting, and in my opinion, one of the most beautiful locations in the world. Full of natural beauty, accessible by public transit, and known for preserving the past—a perfect fit. I love that you can stroll down to the water's edge, hike through a eucalyptus forest, visit the Golden Gate Bridge, or picnic on the parade grounds—all within walking distance of our front doors. My mother had also wisely pointed out the significance of being in a national park, remarking, "Our building, [which] we have refurbished into this amazing museum of my father's life, belongs to the people of the United States of America. ... My dad was kind of everywhere and he was all over the world ... but California was his home and we'd never think of living anyplace else."

Building a state-of-the-art museum with more than 200 screens, listening stations, interactive games and touch points, and contemporary exhibits in a former Army barracks

PAGE 2 Walt with a drawing of Mickey Mouse as Steamboat Willie, 1947

PAGE 4 Walt showing models to Sharon (left) and Diane, c. 1948

OPPOSITE (LEFT TO RIGHT) Jennifer Miller, Lillian Disney, Walter Miller, and Walt Disney aboard the *Mad Tea Party* attraction at Disneyland, c. 1962–3

building, while still preserving its foundational integrity and historic façade, posed a unique challenge. Careful retrofitting and remodeling were required, which included transforming an outdoor courtyard into an enclosed, two-level gallery with a wall of windows providing unmatched views of the San Francisco Bay.

My mother and I both agreed, however, that the most valuable and captivating element in the museum is Walt's voice. From the beginning, our intention was that Walt himself would act as narrator, guiding you through his life as you explore each space. Hours and hours of audio recordings from a series of 1956 interviews with journalist Peter Martin (originally conducted for an article series in the *Saturday Evening Post* and later a book, both authored by my mother) play throughout the galleries and bring Walt's story to life—accompanying the hundreds of drawings, paintings, photographs, artifacts, and contextual historical information.

As important as it was to my mother that the museum showcase who Walt was as a person, a father, a grandfather, a husband, a brother, a boss, and a friend, it was equally critical that his personal story also be prevalent throughout this book—his accomplishments and failures, his innovation and faults. The artifacts in our museum's collection were handpicked to exemplify who Grampa was as a person. Not every object that belonged to Walt was added to the museum's collection, and these heirlooms are incredibly special to my family. My siblings and cousin, Michelle Lund, looked through the special items in our own private collections to share the stories and sentiments behind these objects with you. Featured in this book is my mother's charm bracelet that she received as a present resulting from Walt and Lillian's 1935 travels through Europe that was given to my sister Jennifer Miller Goff (p. 37), Walt's cowboy boots that were given to my sister Tamara Miller (p. 172), and my Aunt Sharon's sixteenth birthday portrait that was in my cousin Michelle's private collection (p. 103). Each family object has been carefully selected not only to preserve our cherished memories, but to demonstrate every distinctive attribute and characteristic that made Walt Disney the Grampa that we knew.

In the summer of 2023, I stepped into the role of President of the Board of Directors of The Walt Disney Family Museum, and am honored to continue contributing to this inspirational space that my mother first imagined so many years ago. My siblings and I all understand the profound responsibility we have in order to continue both our grandparents' and parents' legacies. We personally feel that we owe Grampa so much, not only as grandchildren who admire him, but mostly for what he gave to the world in his short life.

As we celebrate our fifteenth year of operation, I feel great pride in how far our museum has come. We continue to have a strong, collaborative relationship with the Walt Disney Animation Research Library and Walt Disney Archives, providing visitors from around the world with exciting original exhibitions and unique experiences that they can hold on to emotionally—a tangible part of Walt's legacy to learn from and be inspired by. Or, simply, to gain a deeper understanding of who my grandfather was and how he accomplished everything he gave to the world.

Every item featured in this book tells a story—some that are well-known Disney lore, and others that are rarely told—each representing an important brick that helped build a global empire, but also exploring who the person Walt Disney truly was. We not only hope this book will be a piece of The Walt Disney Family Museum you can take home with you, but that you might even discover something new about Walt hidden in these pages.

Walter E. D. Miller

Walter E. D. Miller
President of the Board for The Walt Disney Family Museum and Walt Disney's grandson

FOREWORD

The Walt Disney Family Museum is a nonprofit organization that celebrates the remarkable life story, innovative achievements, and timeless legacy of Walt Disney. Located in San Francisco—just minutes from the iconic Golden Gate Bridge—the museum has welcomed millions of visitors from all over the world since opening on October 1, 2009.

The first question we are often asked is, "Why is the museum in San Francisco?" Though there are interesting threads of Walt's story that intersect with the Bay Area, our museum is here because Diane Disney Miller—Walt's eldest daughter and museum co-founder—lived here. A generous philanthropist and patron of the arts, Diane Disney Miller was a creative force and tireless champion of her father's legacy.

Over the last two decades of her life, Diane undertook an active advocacy to document the life and accomplishments of her father. Many people suggested she write a book, but Diane ultimately decided that a museum would be the most fitting way to tell her father's story. She felt that a state-of-the-art, interactive space with which people of all ages could engage was a more appropriate way to honor her father, the iconic entertainer and innovator.

Diane and her husband, Ron Miller, moved to the San Francisco Bay Area in the mid-1980s, founding Silverado Vineyards in Napa Valley. Diane and her family chose to open the museum in San Francisco so that they could be personally and consistently involved with the construction and governance of the museum.

Perhaps the most unique aspect of Diane's vision for The Walt Disney Family Museum was her desire to chronicle the full story of her father's life and legacy. Diane wanted to share details of not only her father's greatest professional achievements and accolades, but also of his humanity, including the tough periods and personal challenges he faced. "The art is beautiful, but it's more important to get the words," Diane said of the collection. "The truth is so important to me. Not an exaggeration or a beautification of [Dad's] life." Serving as museum co-founder alongside her son, Walter Miller, current President of the Board of Directors, Diane encouraged originality and ingenuity. Beyond being a generous philanthropist and enthusiastic supporter of the arts, Diane was her father's daughter—she had an unrelenting perseverance to accomplish and achieve, carrying on her father's legacy with dignity, grace, and devotion. It was an indescribable honor to work with her.

Following her passing in November 2013, the museum's special exhibition space overlooking the San Francisco Bay was renamed the Diane Disney Miller Exhibition Hall. Ron Miller, former President and CEO of The Walt Disney Company, carried Diane's vision forward, honoring his wife's memory, and providing sage and steady guidance to the museum until his passing in February 2019. Ron had both a great business mind and an extraordinarily creative and intuitive spirit. He was generous and gracious in his leadership and authentically connected with both our museum staff and guests. It was also an extraordinary honor to work closely with Ron over many years.

Though Diane and Ron are no longer with us, their vision is an indelible part of The Walt Disney Family Museum's fabric and has helped shape the past fifteen years. Thanks to the momentum provided by Diane and Ron, and with the guiding inspiration of Diane's father, the torch has now been passed to the next generations of Walt's family, with a Board of Directors consisting of Walt Disney's grandchildren and great-grandchildren: current Board President Walter Miller and Board members Christopher Miller, Tamara Diane Miller, Michelle Lund, Reilly Miller, Haley Scheer, and Charlotte Goff—along with Pat Gallagher and me. We are united in our dedication, and we are determined to carry our institution into the future.

The museum's mission, crafted by Diane, is twofold: to inform present and future generations about the man and, through his story, to inspire them to heed their imagination and persevere in pursuing their goals. Walt once said, "In order to make good in your chosen task, it's important to have someone you want to do it for. The greatest moments in life are not concerned with selfish achievements but rather with the things we do for the people we love ..."

This book was conceived out of love for you, our supporters, fans, and readers. To showcase key objects from the astonishingly comprehensive museum collection, we organized this book by eight chapters that each signify a theme in Walt's rich and multifaceted legacy. For example, "Heart" represents his devotion to his family and focuses on his relationships with the people who loved him and knew him best; "Creativity" highlights Walt's curiosities and passion projects that kept him busy outside of his commitments at the studio; and "Innovation" takes a closer look his experimental and trailblazing contributions to the craft of animated, live-action, and documentary cinema.

At his core, Walt was a storyteller and a visionary. From his humble beginnings, his perseverance through countless challenges was truly staggering. Never one to give up on his dreams, he transformed the world of entertainment forever. Encapsulating this distinct legacy and success in one museum—from his most recognizable characters to technological innovations, his service to his country, his films' exploration and appreciation of diverse cultures, his attention to conservation, and more—is not an easy task. But, as Walt famously said, "It's kind of fun to do the impossible."

Kirsten Komoroske
Executive Director of The Walt Disney Family Museum

OPPOSITE Walt and his staff in front of the multiplane camera, 1951

PART 1
HEART

Beyond the countless achievements and beloved films, it can be easy to forget that there was a person behind the name of The Walt Disney Company. Walt was a loving son, brother, husband, father, and grandfather. Above all else to him, family came first. Thanks to strong family ties and a fondly remembered home life, he dared to dream, create, and explore.

Walt Disney came from humble beginnings. His childhood can perhaps be identified as a classic start to the realization of the American dream. Starting with his grandparents' immigration to Canada—and, later, America—the Disney family established themselves from the ground up.

FLORA CALL AND ELIAS DISNEY'S
WEDDING MEMORABILIA

ON NEW YEAR'S DAY, 1888, Elias and Flora were married in her parents' home in Kismet, Florida. There are unfortunately no photographs from the wedding ceremony, but what remains in the family collection are these special buttons from Flora's wedding dress inlaid terrazzo style with mother of pearl.

Walt's parents were a contrasting couple: Flora was known to be fun-loving; Elias was dutiful, strict, and patriarchal. But their individual work ethic provided a successful partnership. The couple started a hotel in Daytona Beach, Florida, where their first son, Herbert Arthur, was born. After tourism dried up for the year, in 1890 the Disneys moved to Chicago, Illinois. The couple would purchase a plot at what is now 2156 North Tripp Avenue, where they designed and built the home where they would eventually reside. "Mother was the architect. ... [She] drew the plans and ... bought the materials ... Dad was the builder, and see, they worked like a team," recalled Walt's brother, Roy O. Disney.

ABOVE Portrait of Elias and Flora Disney, 1918

RIGHT Buttons from Flora Disney's wedding dress, 1887; miscellaneous materials

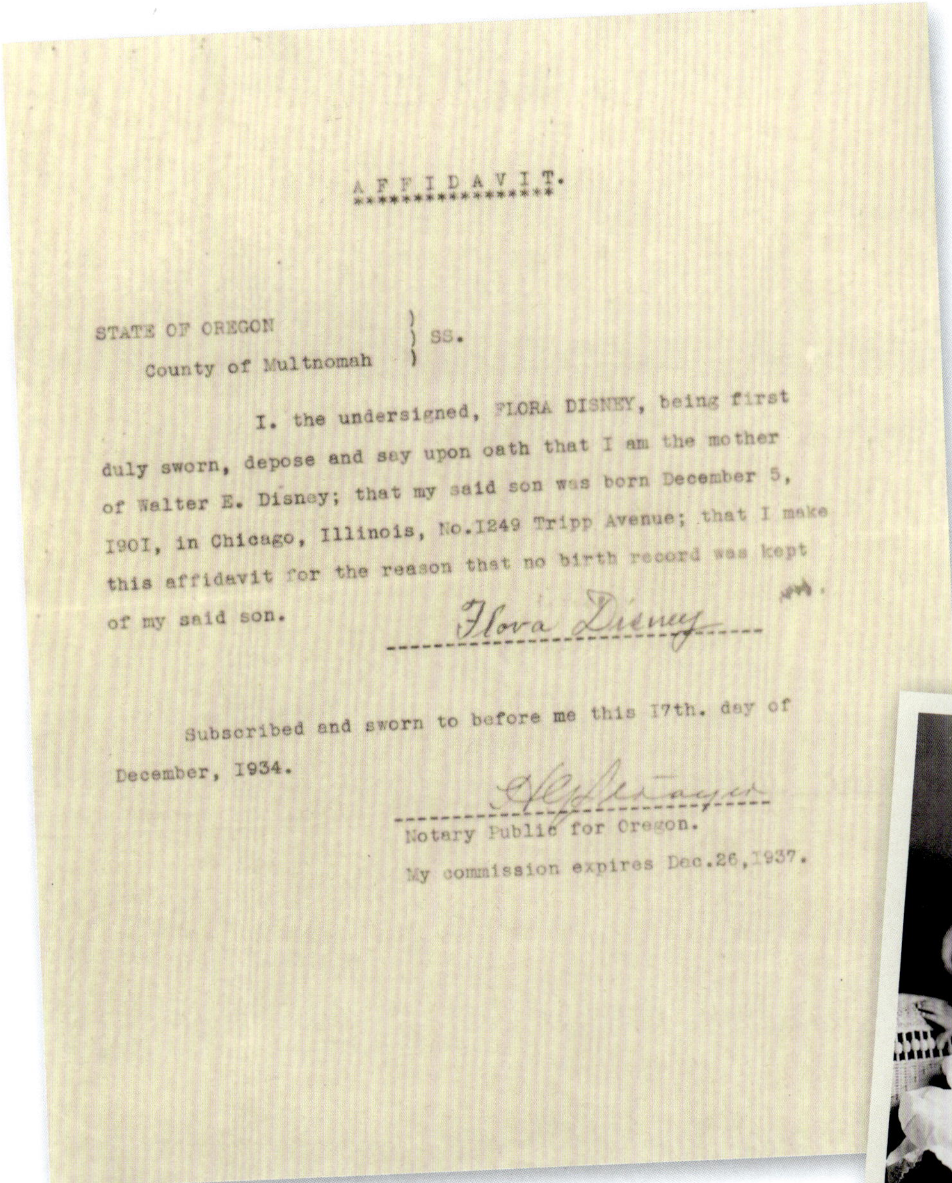

A F F I D A V I T.

STATE OF OREGON)
) SS.
County of Multnomah)

I, the undersigned, FLORA DISNEY, being first duly sworn, depose and say upon oath that I am the mother of Walter E. Disney; that my said son was born December 5, 1901, in Chicago, Illinois, No.1249 Tripp Avenue; that I make this affidavit for the reason that no birth record was kept of my said son.

Flora Disney

Subscribed and sworn to before me this 17th. day of December, 1934.

Notary Public for Oregon.
My commission expires Dec.26,1937.

WALT DISNEY'S
AFFIDAVIT OF BIRTH

IN CHICAGO, THE FAMILY WELCOMED FOUR MORE CHILDREN. First came Raymond Arnold and Roy Oliver, then on December 5, 1901, their fourth son was born: Walter Elias Disney. Two years and a day later, the family welcomed their first and only daughter, Ruth Flora.

When Walt was born, Elias had helped build the St. Paul's Congregational Church and would later become a deacon. "He and the minister were great pals," Walt recalled. "The minister's name was Walter Parr. The minister had a baby coming and my dad had a baby coming. They probably were breaking bread somewhere [and] they said, 'if you name your son after me, I'll name my son after you.' There's somebody around here by the name of Elias Parr and I'm known as Walter after the minister. My dad, he was really feeling good. He gave me the middle name of Elias."

TOP Affidavit from 1934 of Walt's birth on December 5, 1901; handwritten and printed ink on paper

INSET Walt at nine months old, 1902

WALT AND ROY O. DISNEY

CHILDHOOD PHOTOGRAPHS

GROWING UP, Roy would often help take care of his younger siblings Walt and Ruth. Said Walt, "Roy was about eight years old when I was in a baby buggy. It was Roy's chore to push me around." Later, Walt's older brothers joined the military: Herbert and Raymond enlisted in the Army and Roy the Navy. Upon seeing Roy off to The Great War, Walt became determined to serve in some way, though he was only sixteen and too young to officially enlist.

Despite the age difference, Walt and Roy had a very strong bond. This relationship would prove to be very important in 1923, when the two brothers would first go into business together. Roy would later become Walt's business partner, co-founding the Disney Brothers Cartoon Studio, known today as The Walt Disney Company.

Walt recalled, "Roy had faith in me ... I think that Roy has done a lot of things against his better judgment because he felt that I wanted to do it. Most of our arguments and disagreements ... have been because Roy has felt that he had to protect me."

OPPOSITE Walt (seated) and Roy O. Disney, 1917

LEFT Teenage Walt wearing older brother Roy's Navy uniform, 1917

MARCELINE, MISSOURI
PHOTO COLLECTION

IN APRIL 1906, Flora and Elias moved their five children to the small farm town of Marceline, Missouri. Walt was only four at the time, but Elias enlisted his three eldest sons, Herbert, Raymond, and Roy, to work on the farm. They plowed the spring fields and planted sorghum, and lesser amounts of wheat and barley. Walt had lived in Marceline for more than five years, yet that period left more of an impression than any other time in his life. Forty years later, when he built a barn for a workshop on his estate in California, it was a fondly remembered replica of the one he had known in Marceline.

When Walt passed away in 1966, Americans around the nation called for a commemorative stamp celebrating the life of Walt Disney. Postal regulations at the time stated any non-presidential individual honored on a commemorative stamp must have been dead for ten years. However, in the two years since Walt's passing, the support for the stamp's production was overwhelming. The Office of the Postmaster General received letters from Americans around the nation, including California governor Ronald Reagan, actors Fess Parker and John Wayne, and several members of U.S. Congress, urging the postal service to make an exception for Walt.

Marceline, Missouri, was selected as the place to hold the celebration for the release of the commemorative stamp as a way to highlight how much the small town meant to Walt throughout his lifetime. In 1938, Walt wrote, "To tell the truth more things of importance happened to me in Marceline than have happened since–or are likely to in the future." An album of photos, including the selections on this page, was gifted to the Disney family by Rush and Inez Johnson commemorating "Stamp Day" on September 11, 1968, with photos of Walt's 1956 trip to Marceline. The Johnson family hosted Walt and Lillian, along with Roy and Edna, in their home.

Photographs from Marceline, Missouri, photo and document album, 1956; photographs, paper, plastic, and metal

WALT DISNEY
MUNICIPAL PARK

WELCOME BACK
WALT and ROY
UPTOWN
Hamm's BEER
UPTOWN
LIQUOR
DRUGS
MYERS CLOTHING

ELIAS DISNEY'S

PRIZED FIDDLE

WALT RECALLED HIS FATHER, Elias Disney, learned to play the fiddle at an early age. Elias's parents forbade music on religious grounds, which meant to pursue his passion of playing music he would sneak into the forest to practice. Because he had to hide this from his family, Elias played at country dances in other townships. Eventually, his parents caught wind of this and confronted him. At one of these gatherings, in front of everyone, Elias's mother smashed the fiddle and marched him home by the ear.

As a father, Elias struggled to see how his youngest son, Walt, could make a reputable living as a cartoonist. Elias was determined to make a musician out of Walt at a young age, particularly, a violinist. Walt recalled Elias insisting, "Walter is going to be a musician." Even after protests from Walt, Elias insisted, "You have talent, and you ought do it." Elias paid five dollars for a violin from a hock shop and secured lessons for Walt, but Walt resisted. Said Walt, "He never forgave me because he had that five dollars invested in that fiddle."

He continued, "I liked music, but I just had a tin ear. I can't even whistle a tune and stay in pitch. But [my father] was going to make me a violinist. He wouldn't let anybody call him a violinist–he was a fiddler. There was a difference."

OPPOSITE Elias Disney's fiddle and bow, c. 1880; wood, metal, and possibly bone

LEFT Elias Disney's wedding portrait photographed in Daytona Beach, Florida, 1888

ROY O. DISNEY'S
AFFIDAVIT OF HEIRSHIP

ELIAS AND FLORA LIVED to see their two sons start a business together, attain a modest success, and build on that to achieve worldwide recognition. Elias had a seemingly endless capacity for hard work and a tenacity to overcome insurmountable obstacles. At the age of eighty, Elias donned work clothes and helped supervise the carpentry for the building of Walt and Roy's new Burbank studio. Walt remembered, "He was a good dad. He thought of nothing but his family." Walt recalled of his mother Flora, "She was very happy and was very proud of Roy and I and what we'd done." The Disney family's third eldest son, Roy O., had this affidavit signed to attest to all surviving heirs of Elias and Flora.

Flora Call Disney | April 22, 1868 – November 26, 1938

After their success with *Snow White and the Seven Dwarfs* (1937), Walt and Roy moved their parents into a bungalow in North Hollywood, a short distance from Roy's home. On the night of November 26, 1938, a defect in the furnace caused Flora's death by asphyxiation, and Walt and Roy blamed themselves. Walt was sensitive about his mother's death throughout the remainder of his life. Twenty years later, one of his secretaries casually mentioned his mother's death. Walt said sternly, "I don't want that ever brought up in this office again," and he hurried out of the room.

Elias Disney | February 6, 1859 – September 13, 1941

In 1941, Walt made a goodwill visit to South America on behalf of the U.S. government as part of President Franklin Delano Roosevelt's Good Neighbor policy. Walt and his team of hand-picked artists and staff were away for weeks gathering research for film projects that would include *Saludos Amigos* (1943) and *The Three Caballeros* (1945). During their trip, Roy had to break the news via telegram that their father, Elias Disney, had passed away. Elias was eighty-two years old at the time and had never fully recovered from the loss of his beloved Flora. Walt later remarked, "I only wish that Roy and I could have had success sooner, so we could have done more for my mother and father."

BELOW LEFT (left to right) Walt, Elias, and Roy at a celebration for Elias's birthday in Walt's office at The Walt Disney Studios in Burbank, 1940

BELOW RIGHT Flora Disney with her sons (left to right) Walt, Roy, Raymond, and Herbert, c. 1925

OPPOSITE LEFT Walt and Flora, c. 1925

OPPOSITE RIGHT Affidavit and Proof of Heirship of Elias and Flora Disney, 1949; handwritten and printed ink on paper

BOOK 22 PAGE 503

AFFIDAVIT AND PROOF OF HEIRSHIP
OF ELIAS DISNEY AND OF FLORA DISNEY

ATE OF CALIFORNIA)
) SS
UNTY OF LOS ANGELES)

I, ROY O. DISNEY, on oath depose and say:

1. That I am an adult person residing at 4311 Forman nue, North Hollywood, California, and that I am one of the sur- ing children of ELIAS DISNEY and FLORA DISNEY, both of whom are eased, FLORA DISNEY having predeceased ELIAS DISNEY.

2. That said ELIAS DISNEY was married only once and said A DISNEY was married only once, and then to each other, and as sult of said marriage the following children, and no others, born:

Herbert A. Disney, now residing at 1915 Holly Vista,
Los Angeles, California

Raymond A. Disney, now residing at 3912 West Alameda Avenue,
Burbank, California

Roy O. Disney, now residing at 4311 Forman Avenue,
North Hollywood, California

alter E. Disney, now residing at 4053 Woking Way,
Los Angeles 27, California

Ruth Flora Beecher, now residing at 1618 S.E. Morrison Street,
Portland 10, Oregon

3. That all the aforesaid children of ELIAS DISNEY and FLORA DISNEY are now living.

Dated at Burbank, California, October 7, 1949.

Roy O. Disney
Roy O. Disney

On this 7 day of October, 1949, before me, the under- signed Notary Public, personally appeared Roy O. Disney who, being by me first duly sworn, stated that he is the person who subscribed to the foregoing Affidavit; that he has read said affidavit and knows the contents thereof and that the same is true of his own knowledge.

Roy O. Disney
Roy O. Disney

Subscribed and sworn to before me this 7 day of October, 1949.

DOROTHY E. LACHEL NOTARY PUBLIC LOS ANGELES CO. CALIF.

My Commission Expires July 28, 1950
In And For The County Of Los Angeles
State of California

Dorothy E. Lachel
Notary Public in and for the County of Los Angeles, State of California.

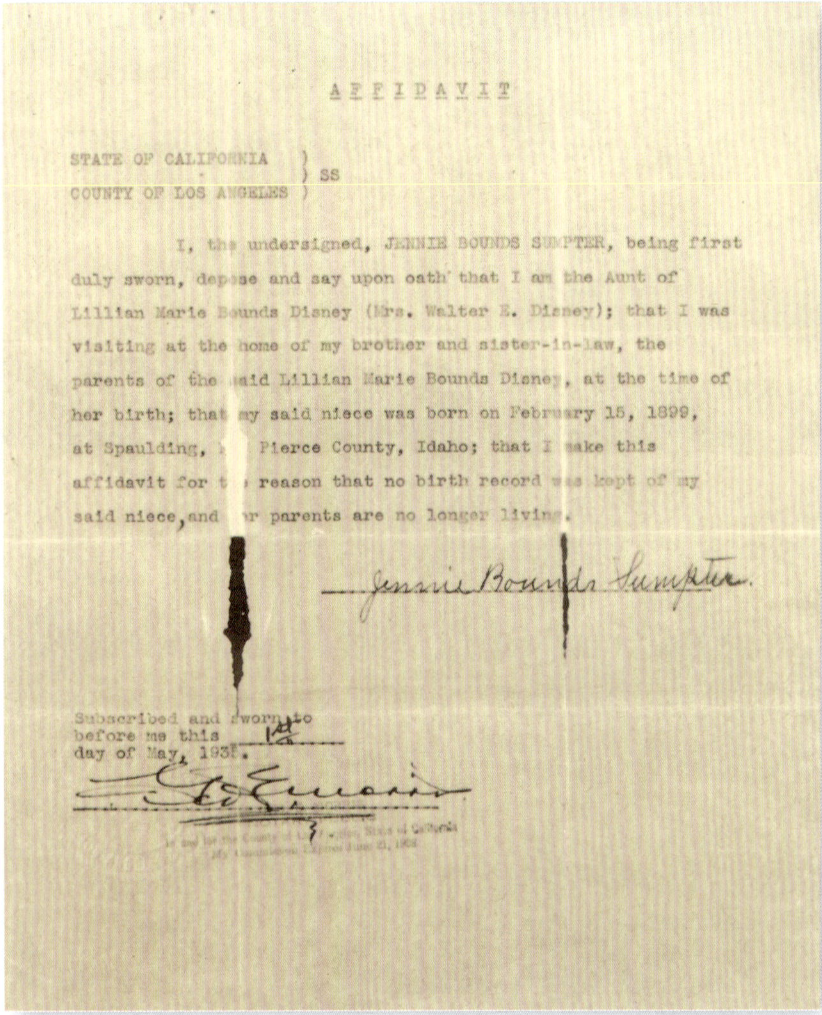

A F F I D A V I T

STATE OF CALIFORNIA)
) SS
COUNTY OF LOS ANGELES)

I, the undersigned, JENNIE BOUNDS SUMPTER, being first duly sworn, depose and say upon oath that I am the Aunt of Lillian Marie Bounds Disney (Mrs. Walter E. Disney); that I was visiting at the home of my brother and sister-in-law, the parents of the said Lillian Marie Bounds Disney, at the time of her birth; that my said niece was born on February 15, 1899, at Spaulding, Pierce County, Idaho; that I make this affidavit for the reason that no birth record was kept of my said niece, and her parents are no longer living.

Jennie Bounds Sumpter

Subscribed and sworn to before me this 1st day of May, 1935.

LILLIAN MARIE BOUNDS
AFFIDAVIT OF BIRTH

THE YOUNGEST OF TEN CHILDREN, Lillian Marie Bounds was born on February 15, 1899, in Spalding, Idaho, to Jeanette Short Bounds and Willard Pehall Bounds. Her father had worked as a scout for General George Crook. He later worked for the U.S. government as a federal marshal on the Nez Perce reservation in Lapwai, Idaho. Willard was also a blacksmith, and Lillian would often remark how much she loved to go by his shop after school. "I used to walk down from my house just to be with him and watch him with the forge, the big flames, and the horses. He made all the equipment, and he would pound the nails used to put the shoes on until they would fit the horses," she recalled.

After finishing high school in Lapwai, Lillian went to business college in Lewiston for two years. She did some secretarial work, though claimed she was "a lousy secretary." Lillian was living and working in Lewiston when her father died. At the time, she and her mother were living with her brother, Sid. Eventually, Lillian decided to head to Los Angeles to be with her sister, Hazel.

TOP Affidavit from 1935 of Jennie Bounds Sumpter stating Lillian Bounds' birth date of February 1899; handwritten and printed ink on paper

BOTTOM Portrait of young Lillian Bounds (center) with her sister Hazel and brother Lloyd, c. 1905

WALT AND LILLIAN'S

MARRIAGE CERTIFICATE

WALT AND LILLIAN (fondly called "Lilly" by her closest friends and family) had met when she was hired at the Disney Brothers Cartoon Studio as an inker and painter. The first studio employee, Kathleen Dollard, told Lillian, "I have a job for you, but I am telling you about it on one condition: don't marry the boss."

Lillian started inking and painting black and white cels for the Alice Comedies and was later promoted to be Walt's first official secretary. Walt would frequently offer to chauffeur Lillian and Kathleen to ensure the women arrived home safely. As the story goes, Walt always dropped Lillian off last, even though her home was nearer.

When they started courting in earnest, Lillian remembered, "He was fun even if he didn't have a nickel. We would go to see a picture show or take a drive. We would drive up to Santa Barbara sometimes. He was always talking about what he was going to do." On July 13, 1925, Walt Disney married Lillian Bounds at her brother's home in Lewiston, Idaho.

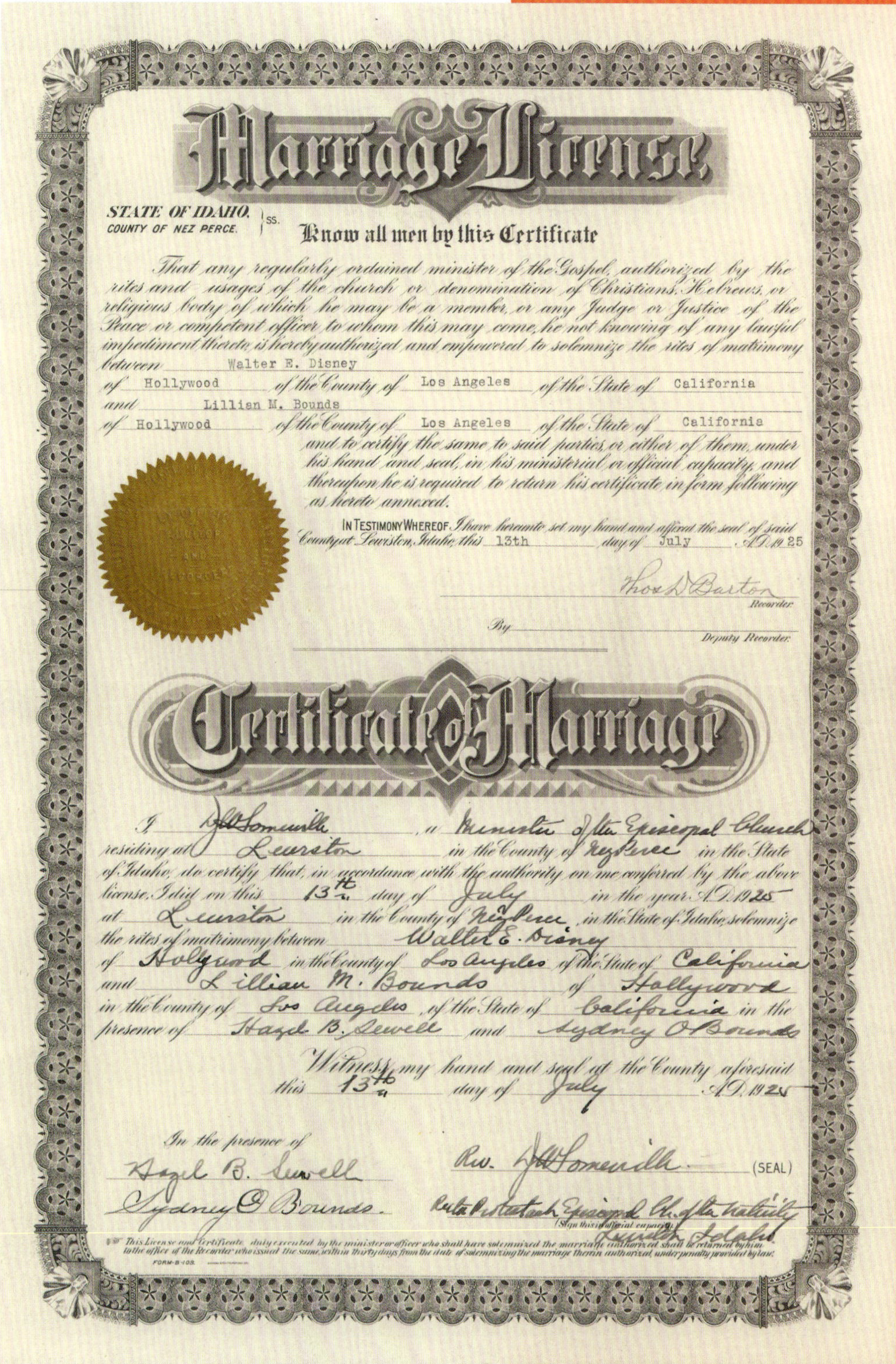

Marriage License

STATE OF IDAHO, COUNTY OF NEZ PERCE. } SS.

Know all men by this Certificate

That any regularly ordained minister of the Gospel, authorized by the rites and usages of the church or denomination of Christians, Hebrews, or religious body of which he may be a member, or any Judge or Justice of the Peace or competent officer to whom this may come, he not knowing of any lawful impediment thereto, is hereby authorized and empowered to solemnize the rites of matrimony between Walter E. Disney of Hollywood of the County of Los Angeles of the State of California and Lillian M. Bounds of Hollywood of the County of Los Angeles of the State of California and to certify the same to said parties, or either of them, under his hand and seal, in his ministerial or official capacity, and thereupon he is required to return his certificate in form following as hereto annexed.

IN TESTIMONY WHEREOF, I have hereunto set my hand and affixed the seal of said County at Lewiston, Idaho, this 13th day of July A.D. 1925

Thos D Barton
Recorder.

By ______ Deputy Recorder.

Certificate of Marriage

I, [illegible], a Minister of the Episcopal Church residing at Lewiston in the County of Nez Perce in the State of Idaho, do certify that, in accordance with the authority on me conferred by the above license, I did on this 13th day of July in the year A.D. 1925 at Lewiston in the County of Nez Perce, in the State of Idaho, solemnize the rites of matrimony between Walter E. Disney of Hollywood in the County of Los Angeles of the State of California and Lillian M. Bounds of Hollywood in the County of Los Angeles, of the State of California in the presence of Hazel B. Sewell and Sydney O Bounds

Witness my hand and seal at the County aforesaid this 13th day of July A.D. 1925

In the presence of
Hazel B. Sewell
Sydney O Bounds

Rev. [illegible] (SEAL)
[illegible] Episcopal Ch. of the Nativity, Lewiston, Idaho
(Sign this in official capacity)

This License and Certificate duly executed by the minister or officer who shall have solemnized the marriage authorized shall be returned by him to the office of the Recorder who issued the same, within thirty days from the date of solemnizing the marriage therein authorized, under penalty provided by law.

FORM-B-103.

LEFT Walt Disney and Lillian Bounds posing on their wedding day, July 13, 1925

RIGHT Marriage License and Certificate of Walter E. Disney and Lillian Bounds, July 13, 1925; handwritten and printed ink on paper

LILLIAN'S OSCAR®
CHARM BRACELET

ABOVE Oscar charm bracelet, 1954; gold

BELOW LEFT Walt and Lillian at the Golden Horseshoe Saloon at Disneyland Park on their thirtieth wedding anniversary, July 13, 1955

BELOW RIGHT Walt holding Lillian's Oscar charm bracelet, 1954

IN 1954, Walt was able to purchase miniature Oscar statuettes that represented his many wins and decided to give them to his wife, Lillian, to acknowledge the role she had played in his professional success. He acquired twenty 18-karat gold charms, each engraved with the name of the film for which he was awarded, representing the awards he had received to that time (he would receive thirty-two in his lifetime, the current record holder for most individual honors). Walt envisioned having a necklace made from these charms, but Lillian said she would prefer a bracelet.

Perhaps most humorously, the bracelet was also a way for Walt to get himself out of the "doghouse," so to speak. Walt had been nominated for several Academy Awards® in 1954 and didn't think he'd win any, so he told Lillian it wouldn't be worth the trouble for her to attend that year's ceremony. Of course, Walt ended up winning four Oscars—more than anyone had won in a single evening to date—so Lillian, ever-supportive, was upset she hadn't attended. Thus, the "Oscar bracelet" made the perfect gift for many reasons. According to their daughter, Diane, Lillian wore the bracelet often and with great pride.

LEFT Walt wearing the Langley watch while on the phone, c. 1939

BELOW Hamilton Watch Company, Walt's Langley cuff watch, 1934; metal and leather

WALT'S LEATHER-CUFFED
HAMILTON WATCH

LILLIAN GAVE THIS Hamilton Watch Company timepiece to Walt as a Christmas present in 1934. The watch is a "Langley" design fashioned with 14-karat gold, a manual hand-wound movement, solid gold numbers on the dial, and 17 jewels, which was produced from 1930 through 1934. Named for the early American aviation pioneer Samuel Langley, it was sold in 1934 for ninety dollars. This design was advertised as "a distinguished design for the man of today." Walt's watch was originally fastened with a black pigskin band. By the 1940s, Walt had customized it with a brown leather cuff.

"This is the only watch I remember [my dad] wearing and [it] was distinctive because of the leather cuff. The inscription on the back reads, 'To Walt from Lilly 12.25.34,'" said their daughter Diane. According to Diane, Lillian collected clocks, so it seems fitting she would gift Walt a wristwatch. The family home had many clocks, and from time to time a clock winder would come to the home and wind them.

THIS PAGE Bronzed hat given to Lillian by Walt, 1941; bronze

OPPOSITE Lillian, Walt, and Diane at the Rose Parade, January 2, 1939

GIFT FROM WALT TO LILLIAN

BRONZED HAT

WALT SHARED A LIFETIME OF LAUGHTER not only with the world, but also with his family and friends. The stories of him and his personal effects echo the supportive, loving relationship that Walt and Lillian shared—it's clear that much of their relationship was punctuated by good humor. Walt's beloved hats were often the subject of laughter and fun. Much to Lillian's dissatisfaction, Walt often wore hats at a jaunty, rakish angle. When Lillian asked Walt to "fix" his hat, he would often respond by crushing the hat on his head, which would cause Lillian to playfully take the hat from him altogether. In an ode to this back and forth, Walt presented Lillian with a very special gift on her birthday, February 15, 1941.

At first, Lillian thought Walt had given her a lovely arrangement of orchids, but, when she lifted the flowers from their "vase," she found Walt's favorite hat. The crown had been pressed into the shape of a heart and the entire hat had been preserved in bronze. Her birthday gift was "The Hat Bronzed with Love." Walt had finally done what Lilly had asked—he permanently *fixed* his hat! For Walt, the bronzing of his hat symbolized the ways in which his and Lilly's laughter and love withstood the test of time.

"Some years ago, I had been hounding [Walt] about a disreputable old hat he insisted on wearing ... Finally, the disreputable hat vanished ... But it turned up again on my birthday. Walt had it copper-plated ... and then filled it with brown orchids. It hangs in our projection room, and I feel very sentimental about it."

—LILLIAN DISNEY

VICTORIAN-INSPIRED
DISNEYLAND APARTMENT

DURING DEVELOPMENT, Walt had always assumed he would one day need a regular place to rest and sleep in Disneyland. The Park was built while he was in the middle of producing *Lady and the Tramp* (1955), which meant countless car journeys between a semi-completed park in Anaheim, The Walt Disney Studios in Burbank, and his Carolwood Drive home in Los Angeles. "He'd spend long mornings at the studio, then out in Anaheim in the afternoons and back—it's a long drive," recalled Walt's daughter, Diane Disney Miller. The decision was made: Walt would have a small apartment built near Main Street, U.S.A. He would be able to work and rest there, and his family could also use it as a base while visiting or exploring Disneyland.

Emile Kuri, an Academy Award®-winning set decorator, was selected to decorate the apartment in a Victorian theme, a favorite era of Walt and Lillian's, replete with accents of the era's famed cranberry glass. Kuri's work would enchant guests for years to come, immortalizing the Disneys' Victorian vision. Once the Disneyland opening frenzy had calmed a little, Walt settled in. Walt's grandchildren fondly remember spending their evenings in the cranberry-colored hideaway, listening to adventurous sounds drifting through the landscaping from the nearby *Jungle Cruise* attraction.

LEFT Disneyland apartment furniture on display at The Walt Disney Family Museum

RIGHT Walt and Lillian with Joanna, Tamara, and Jennifer Miller in the Disneyland apartment, c. 1963

ABOVE Polaroid photobooth photographs of Walt and Lillian Disney, c. 1957

WALT AND LILLIAN

PHOTOBOOTH IMAGES

THESE INTIMATE PHOTOS OF WALT AND LILLIAN SHOW a side of the two that few have seen other than close friends and family. Far from the buttoned-up businessman and wife of a studio head, here we see two people deeply in love and expressing their playful side, vamping for the camera in various poses.

Diane remembered, "Mother and Dad were somewhere—I forget, I think it might have been New Orleans. I received a long hotel envelope in the mail from them with no note, just these photo-booth shots, which I love."

Lillian shared in the 1953 article, "I Live with a Genius," from *McCall's* magazine about her marriage to Walt, "I wouldn't have missed one minute of the 27 years I have been married to Walt Disney. I'm proud of my husband and what he has done—but I'm even prouder that along the way, in bad times and good, he has never lost his sense of humor or his zest for life."

WALT WITH HIS DAUGHTERS

TREASURED PHOTOGRAPHS

WALT AND LILLIAN INITIALLY STRUGGLED to start a family, but on December 18, 1933, Lillian gave birth to a baby girl, Diane Marie Disney. Diane explains, "Mother had miscarried twice before I was born and once after I came. Her doctor warned her against trying again. Wanting to have a larger family and for me not to be an only child, they decided to adopt a daughter. Shortly after my third birthday at the very end of December 1936, my sister Sharon came into our home."

Walt was adamant that "a man should never neglect his family for business" and rarely brought work home. He was a big family man, who especially loved spending quality time with Diane and Sharon every Sunday, which they dubbed "Daddy's Day." During the week, he made a point to drive the girls to school each morning until they were old enough to drive themselves. Walt recalled, "I never brought my family much in on the studio and things. I kept them very free of the studio. I've lived with it too much and I just did not want to live with it at home. I tried to set up my home as something apart."

TOP Walt holding a kitten with daughters Diane (left) and Sharon, c. 1945

BOTTOM Walt reading to daughters Sharon (left) and Diane, c. 1940

DIANE AND SHARON'S

WEDDING PHOTOS

DIANE DISNEY MET RONALD MILLER on a blind date after a college football game. Ron was a towering football player for the University of Southern California. Walt and Lillian had not particularly liked anyone Diane had been serious about before, but that changed when they met Ron. Diane and Ron picked the date for their wedding, which was held on May 9, 1954, in a small church in Santa Barbara. Walt led Diane down the aisle, and when the minister asked, "Who gives this woman to be married?" Diane heard a sob come from her father. She described, "I turned around and Daddy was standing back there, tears running down his cheeks. I squeezed his hand, and he gave me a soulful look." The pair giggled through their vows and after the ceremony Diane was picked up off her feet by her new groom.

While posing for this photo of Ron and Diane, Walt stood on his tiptoes to lessen the gap between himself and his new six-foot, five-inch son-in-law. The wedding cake had the Disney touch, too—it was designed by Disney artist Mary Blair. The two figures on the top depicted Diane in Levi's and a USC shirt, with Ron in Bermuda shorts and bare feet, wearing a football helmet and holding a football.

In 1958, friends arranged a date for Sharon with Robert "Bob" Brown, a designer with the Charles Luckman architectural firm. Bob had come from a conservative family in Kansas City and was taken by surprise by the humorous antics of the Disney family. Bob eventually became accustomed to the Disney family's unorthodox ways, and after a year-and-a-half of dating he proposed to Sharon. "Well, she's your problem now, Bob," Walt comedically told the bridegroom. Bob and Sharon were married in Pacific Palisades on May 10, 1959. To no one's surprise, Walt cried giving away his youngest daughter.

BELOW LEFT Walt with Ron and Diane at their wedding, May 9, 1954

BELOW RIGHT Sharon and Walt with Diane and Ron on their wedding day, May 9, 1954

OPPOSITE Walt and Bob Brown kiss Sharon at her wedding, May 10, 1959

WALT'S WORLD WAR I

48-STAR AMERICAN FLAG

THIS FLAG WAS GIVEN TO WALT by Harriet Alice Howell, a professor of elocution at the University of Nebraska, in the early 1940s. During World War I she volunteered as a canteen worker for the American Red Cross and met young Walt. This flag flew over their Red Cross camp. Alice once wrote to Walt, saying, "I have a deeply cherished wish that each year on December fifth, at least, this flag may wave over the Disney lot." Walt's daughters, Diane and Sharon, ensured this prized flag was draped over the upstairs railing of the entrance hall of their Woking Way home on his birthday each year.

This 48-star American flag had become the official flag of the United States on July 4, 1912, when New Mexico and Arizona were admitted to the Union. President Taft issued an executive order on June 24 of that year, establishing the new proportions of the flag. This version of the flag flew for 47 years, longer than any previous American flag. It lasted through two World Wars and a total of eight Presidents. In 1959, a 49th star was added with Alaska's admission to the union, and the 50-star flag that flies today was introduced in 1960, when Hawaii was admitted.

COLLECTION OF MINIATURE

SHAKESPEARE BOOKS

WALT GAVE THIS COLLECTION of thirty-six miniature books of William Shakespeare's complete works to his eldest daughter, Diane, for her eighteenth birthday. This special gift represents his passion for miniatures as well as his love of books. For this book set, it is possible to read the full text—though you might need a magnifying glass. Walt also purchased a set for himself. These differ from Diane's set and are bound in red leather with a simple gold embossing of the title on the front cover.

William Shakespeare and Walt Disney would be called the greatest storytellers of their eras, so it makes sense that Walt would be drawn to the Bard of Avon's work. Walt never directly adapted any Shakespearean works, but there are a few Shakespearean references in Walt's films. For example, in *Trick or Treat* (1952), Witch Hazel quotes, "Double, double, toil and trouble. Fire burn and cauldron bubble," riffing on the famous passage from *Macbeth* to Donald Duck's nephews. Her broomstick is named Beelzebub, another *Macbeth* reference. In *The Absent-Minded Professor* (1961), Ned Brainard's rival, Professor Shelby Ashton, quotes from *Hamlet*: "As the Bard says, 'That he is mad, 'tis true, 'tis true, 'tis pity, and pity 'tis 'tis true.'" When Betsy Carlisle attempts to quiet him, he remarks, "Well, if that's what she thinks of Shakespeare ..."

"Mom loved to read and was an avid reader from a very young age. The little Shakespeare collection of miniature books was a focal point in our home and one that tragically we could not keep our little hands off."

—TAMARA MILLER, *GRANDDAUGHTER OF WALT DISNEY*

OPPOSITE American flag with 48 stars that was flown over the Red Cross canteen where Walt served in France, c. 1918; fabric with metal

LEFT Set of Shakespeare miniature books in rotating bookcase; wood, leather, and printed ink on paper

DIANE'S

BRAZILIAN DOLL

PRIOR TO THE UNITED STATES' ENTRY INTO WORLD WAR II, President Roosevelt initiated the Good Neighbor policy to strengthen ties between the country and the republics of Central and South America. To encourage goodwill, Hollywood producers were asked by the government to incorporate Latin American themes and talent into their films and asked Walt to undertake a personal tour as well. Walt responded enthusiastically to this appeal. In the fall of 1941, he, Lillian, and a handpicked group of studio personnel embarked on a goodwill tour of South America, where they gathered artistic impressions of Brazil, Argentina, Chile, and other countries for use in a series of Good Neighbor films.

After months away, Lillian and Walt returned to their daughters with gifts in hand. Diane received a Lenci Doll Company doll depicting popular Brazilian actress Carmen Miranda that stood thirty-six inches tall, which at the time was around the height of eight-year-old Diane. Sharon in turn received a Baiana doll. Internationally, Carmen Miranda popularized Baiana style and became known for her fruit-adorned headwrap.

RIGHT Lenci, Diane's gifted Carmen Miranda doll, 1941; fabric

OPPOSITE Diane's gifted bracelet with charms from Walt and Lillian's travels, 1935; enamel on metal

DIANE'S SOUVENIR EUROPEAN TRAVEL
CHARM BRACELET

IN THE SUMMER OF 1935, Walt and his brother Roy, along with their wives, set sail for a two-month trip to Europe. There the group traveled through the United Kingdom, France, Germany, Austria, Switzerland, and Italy. Walt had been working intensely on the development of *Snow White and the Seven Dwarfs* (1937) and was showing signs of needing a break from his animation studio. On the trip, Walt mixed business and pleasure, attending press events, meeting with dignitaries and artists, and touring historical landmarks.

Walt spent an abundance of his time sourcing books from many places he visited. All in all, he had 335 books shipped back from his travels, with a majority of them to be used as reference material for his artists at the studio. Walt and Lillian also shopped for charms to fill out a bracelet for their two-year-old daughter, Diane.

This special bracelet documents the Disney's 1935 European vacation highlighting some of the significant stops they made along the way. The charms represent the following (from left to right): an amethyst ring (gifted to Diane from Walt in celebration of her birth); the Lucerne, Switzerland, flag; Tirol (Tyrol), Austria, flag; St. Christopher (representing safe travel and protection); the Vatican City crest; flag of France; symbol of the Munich Monk; Paris, France, coat of arms; Salzberg, Austria, crest; and the flag of England.

HAPPY
41

THE DISNEY GRANDKIDS

PHOTO COLLECTION

BELOW Walt on a train with Christopher Miller at Disneyland, 1956

OPPOSITE TOP Walt with Joanna (left) and Tamara Miller in the Disneyland Parade of Toys, 1960

OPPOSITE BOTTOM Diane and Sharon with their children, 1966

WALT WOULD ULTIMATELY become a grandfather of ten. His daughters, Diane and Sharon, had seven and three children, respectively. As is clear from the family photograph collection, Walt took great delight with his grandchildren.

Walt was a proud grandfather and would often take his grandchildren with him to Disneyland. For the Christmas parade, Walt insisted on having his grandchildren accompany him in the car riding through the Park. Walt's eldest grandson, Chris, remembers, "There were at least two occasions where Grampa recruited myself and my oldest sister, Joanna, to accompany him on a Main Street Disneyland parade. I was sitting in the car next to him ... often with his arm around us, I think to sort of coddle us a bit—but I was petrified driving down the street staring at all these adoring people that were probably mostly looking at my grandfather but seemingly looking at me. I think my grandfather wanted us in the parade because he wanted to show us off. He was proud of his grandchildren. I think he also wanted to share with us the sensation of the adulation that he experienced and to be able to see or feel a little bit of what it was like to have throngs of people excited about your appearance on Main Street, U.S.A."

THE DISNEY FAMILY'S SEAWORLD TRIP

PHOTO MEMORIES

IN THE SUMMER OF 1965, Diane accompanied her husband Ron to Paris, France, for a weeklong business trip, and their children headed to their grandparents' house. Their eldest, Christopher "Chris," was away at summer camp, so Joanna, Tamara, Jennifer, Walter, and Ronald Jr. were looked after by Walt and Lillian. According to Diane, "Dad decided that he wanted to see SeaWorld and Vacation Village in San Diego to get ideas for the new Florida Disneyland they were planning." Walt was equipped with his Kodak Instamatic Camera, which the grandkids often turned on their beloved grandfather.

Walter Miller remembers: "I recall massive tortoises that Jenny and I got to ride and get on top. They were like Volkswagens. I'm reminded when I look at the photograph, the only photograph I ever took of my grandpa, which is here ... I think I'm getting lower and lower and lower, and the picture is of my grandpa—it's him just about on his knees, and he's got little sandwiches in his hand ... you can see his little sandwiches there, so it must have been about lunchtime. ... He knew where the camera was with his experience in filmmaking and it's a great shot. I love it."

RIGHT Walt during a trip to San Diego, photograph by Walter Miller, 1965

OPPOSITE Christopher Miller, red crayon drawing, c. 1961; crayon on paper

CHRIS MILLER

RED CRAYON DRAWING

THIS DRAWING, rendered in red crayon on paper, was made circa 1961 by Walt's eldest grandson, Chris. It was a treasured drawing Walt stored away in his valet box. Chris loved to draw and was encouraged by his grandfather from a young age to improve his artistic abilities. Chris remembers, "He was an artist himself, of course, and he'd tell me how to improve my technique. I remember him showing me how to draw effective-looking smoke. ... He was always there—and he took a big interest in my developing artistic skills." He continues, "There was a time when he would [play] a little game where he would take a scribble and turn it into something recognizable. From that I would make something recognizable out of the scribble. Like, add ears to it, eyes to it, etcetera. This blob of marks suddenly became something identifiable."

WALTER ELIAS DISNEY MILLER'S

CIGAR BIRTH ANNOUNCEMENT

WALT'S VALET BOX that was housed on his bathroom dresser held many treasures of the special moments from his life. This Partagás cigar announced the birth of Walt's grandson, Walter Elias Disney Miller.

In 1961, Walt wrote to his sister Ruth: "I don't know if you had heard about the BIG news ... the birth on Tuesday, November 14, of Walter Elias Disney Miller. Diane finally decided to name one of her sons for me, and I'm thrilled to have a male heir bearing my name."

This Cuban Partagás celebratory cigar is notable because it would be the last year that Partagás cigars were produced in Cuba. Due to the Cuban Revolution, Partagás was controlled by the Cuban government and the family that previously owned the company launched a competing cigar line under the Partagás name outside of Cuba. Disney illustrator and animator Sam McKim told Walter Miller, "I remember your grandpa was so excited when you were born, he was handing out all these cigars." When Walter was around ten years old, Lillian Disney presented him with a special keepsake: a box of cigars bearing the birth announcement. This is the only cigar that remains from that box.

TOP Walt pushing Joanna (left) and Chris Miller in an *Autopia* attraction vehicle, 1962

BOTTOM *Autopia* attraction vehicle, c. 1955; metal and miscellaneous materials

OPPOSITE Partagás Cigar announcing Walter E. D. Miller's birth, 1961; metal and tobacco

CHRIS MILLER'S *AUTOPIA* CAR

AS A YOUNG BOY, Walt's eldest grandson, Chris Miller, was interested in automobiles. Needless to say, his favorite attraction at Disneyland was *Autopia,* a miniature freeway attraction featuring sleek gas-powered cars with steering wheels, foot pedals, and road signs. On a trip to the Disney Studios circa 1962, Walt presented eight-year-old Chris a bright red, gas-powered *Autopia* car with his name on the license plate. "It was beyond exciting, almost unbelievable. That car became one of my favorite weekend activities," Chris recalled. "[It] was about as much fun as you could have as kids. The Disney studio [was] an enormous *Autopia*, the buildings and the streets were life size. I would drive on the backlot on weekends, when there was virtually, maybe nobody there, and pretty much have the run of the streets. [On] the backlot sets, we would drive that *Autopia* [car] on dirt roads, paved roads, throughout the large parking lot. My red *Autopia* car was the first car I ever drove."

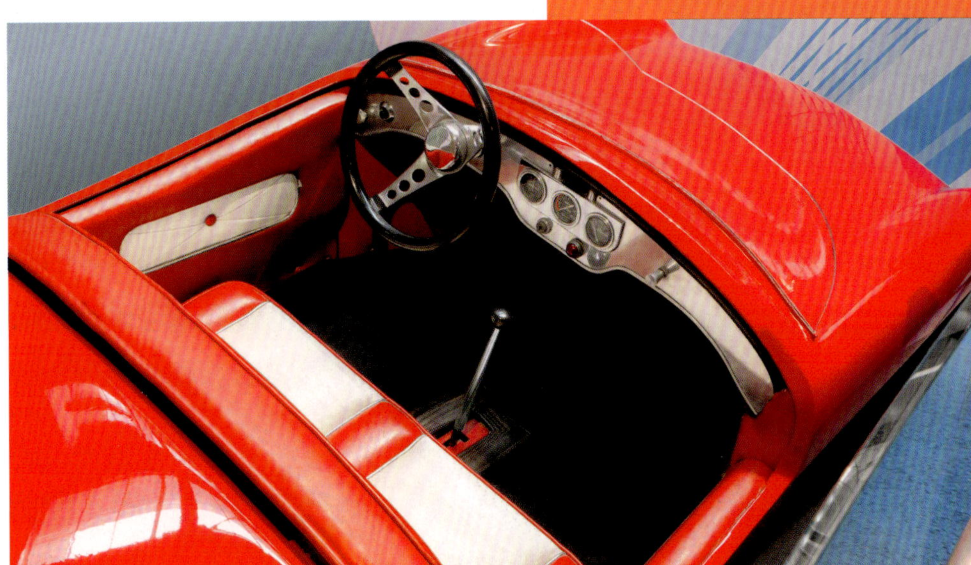

WALT'S FAVORITES

LIST OF FOODS FOR "FOU-FOU"

THELMA PEARL HOWARD started working as a live-in housekeeper and cook at the Disney family's Carolwood home in 1951. For the next thirty years she took care of Walt, Lillian, their children, and grandchildren. "She cleaned the house daily, fed us all breakfast, dinner, and sometimes lunch, and did the laundry perfectly," Diane Disney Miller shared. "She was a superb cook. Her pies were the best. She would dash out into the garden, gather an assortment of flowers, and place charming little arrangements around the house. She moved at the speed of light ... and was a great sports fan. She knew all Hollywood's and the world's gossip and had a stack of movie magazines handy."

Walt referred to Thelma as "the real-life Mary Poppins." Since Walt's eldest grandson Chris couldn't pronounce her name, he and his siblings referred to her as "Fou-Fou." Chris recalled, "I remember [Grampa and Fou-Fou] getting along quite unlike most domestic help and their employers. He was extremely respectful and appreciative of the way she involved herself in our lives."

Walt ate very simply. He liked basic food and loved chili. One day Walt came to the kitchen and handed a list to Thelma, saying, "Here's a list of things I like to eat." That two-page list survived through the decades and was found in an old *LIFE* magazine in the "Maid's Room" that had seen several occupants at the Carolwood home since Thelma's retirement.

RIGHT Thelma Pearl "Fou-Fou" Howard helping at a birthday party with Walter Miller, c. 1964

OPPOSITE List of Walt's favorite foods, c. 1960; handwritten ink on paper

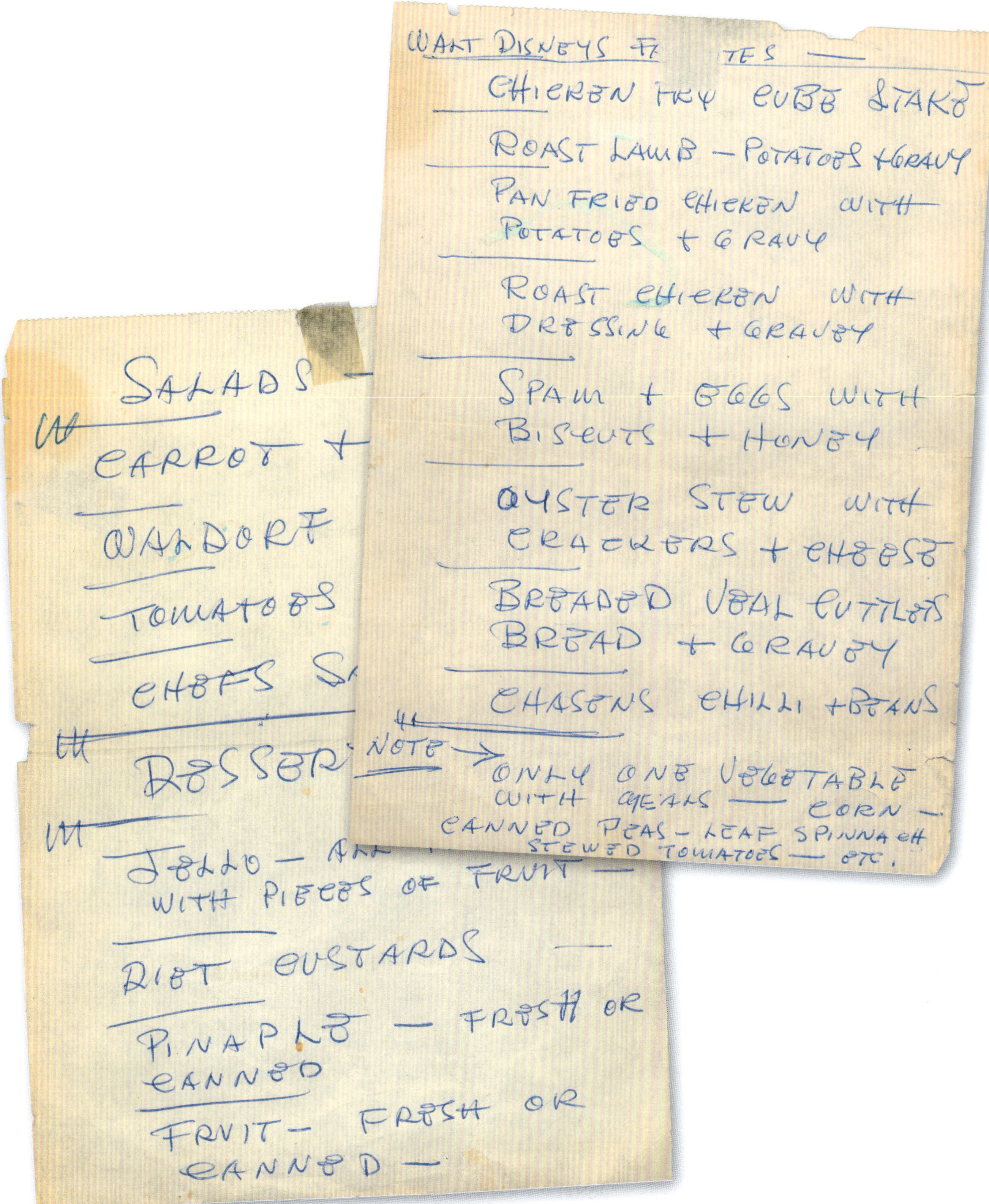

WALT DISNEYS F[illegible]TES —

CHICKEN FRY CUBE STAKE

ROAST LAMB — POTATOES + GRAVY

PAN FRIED CHICKEN WITH
POTATOES + GRAVY

ROAST CHICKEN WITH
DRESSING + GRAVEY

SPAM + EGGS WITH
BISCUITS + HONEY

OYSTER STEW WITH
CRACKERS + CHEESE

BREADED VEAL CUTLETS
BREAD + GRAVEY

CHASENS CHILLI + BEANS

NOTE → ONLY ONE VEGETABLE
WITH MEALS — CORN —
CANNED PEAS — LEAF SPINNACH
STEWED TOMATOES — ETC.

SALADS —

CARROT + [illegible]

WALDORF

TOMATOES

CHEFS SA[illegible]

DESSERT[illegible]

JELLO — A[illegible]
WITH PIECES OF FRUIT —

DIET CUSTARDS —

PINAPLE — FRESH OR
CANNED

FRUIT — FRESH OR
CANNED —

GIFT FROM WALT'S STAFF

METAL OUTHOUSE CLOCK

THIS METAL OUTHOUSE FEATURES a square-faced Art Deco New Haven clock inside. On the doormat is engraved, "Walt from his staff 1930." This thoughtful and humorous gift showcases the relationship he shared with his employees. "Walt was an extraordinary man, and I felt very close to him and a lot of us did," animator Marc Davis recalled. "He looked at us not so much like we were employees, we were people to create with."

Known to be frugal in handing out compliments, if a given work met Walt's standards he would often simply remark, "That'll work." He pushed his employees to not only be critical of their work but when faced with a problem he expected them to figure out a way to improve it or find a solution. He wanted positive thinkers. Story artist Floyd Norman observes, "I think Walt respected people who disagreed with him. He would test people to see if they could defend what they believed in."

Songwriter Richard Sherman remembered, "Walt loved to work in teams. We would have many meetings where an entire group of people [got] together: story [artists], animators, songwriters, art background people and script writers all back together in one room [to] talk about the project. And he liked to have everyone contribute their ideas."

TOP Outhouse clock given to Walt from staff at The Walt Disney Studios, 1930; metal and wood

BOTTOM Walt in a story meeting for *The Grasshopper and the Ants* (1934)

OPPOSITE Coast Guard award for *Men Against the Arctic* (1955), 1956; brass on wood

GREENLAND CRUISES

COAST GUARD AWARD

THIS COAST GUARD BELL was presented to Walt in 1956 for distinctive achievement in the production of his Academy Award®-winning featurette *Men Against the Arctic* (1955). The bell was from the *Greenland Cruise* (a U.S. Coast Guard Arctic survey boat) and was engraved and mounted on a wooden base with a woven rope attached to a clapper. *Men Against the Arctic* documents how icebreakers—specially constructed ships built by the U.S. Coast Guard—must break through heavy Arctic ice packs in an annual mission.

This nautical bell was often rung by Walt's secretaries, at 12:30 p.m. to let him know it was time for lunch. Each evening secretary Tommie Wilck prepared a calendar of the following day's appointments for Walt. She tried to keep him on schedule, and one day when he continued talking with visitors past the 12:30 p.m. lunchtime, she rang the ship's bell. Walt was amused, and instructed her to sound the bell every day at lunchtime.

Walt always appreciated and relied on the work done by his secretaries throughout the years. He told his daughter Diane, "They will either help you get things done or they can prevent things from getting done."

"Only through the talent, the labor, and the dedication of the staff could any Disney project get off the ground."

—WALT

PART 2

DETERMINATION

As Walt ventured into the animation business, he never forgot his humble beginnings. The values instilled by his midwestern upbringing would help him form relationships that would bolster his later successes and prepare him for a life creating entertainment for the public.

While Walt experienced hardships early in his life and career, it was his determination for success that prevailed throughout his life. "All the adversity I've had in my life, all my troubles and obstacles have strengthened me," he said. These objects will help to illustrate how early failures and hardships led some of his greatest achievements.

THE VOICE

THE
TINY VOICE
McKINLEY'S SMALLEST PAPER
VOL1 — JUNE 1918 — NO23
1
I HAVE THE LAND YOU FURNISH THE HELP
UNCLE SAM
S P O R T S
3.
KAISER
SCENE 1
BANG
BANG
KAISER
THREE CHEERS
SCENE 2
4
E D I T O R I A L
5
PLAYING KEEP AWAY
VICTORY
KAISER
ALLIES
IN ORDER THAT WE MAY KEEP IT ALL THE TIME — BUY - SAVE + SERVE —
C O M I C S
6.
I AM TOO FAT TO FIGHT AND I GUESS THERE IS NOTHING I CAN DO TO HELP WIN THIS WAR
WHY DON'T YOU STOP EATING SO MUCH AND SAVE FOOD FOR THE BOYS OVER THERE, AND YOU WILL REDUCE SO YOU CAN FIGHT
I NEVER THOUGHT OF THAT
BUY WAR SAVING STAMPS AND HELP WIN THIS WAR.
APOLIGIES TO ORR
WALTER DISNEY EDITOR

WALT'S

EARLY CARTOONS

WHEN WALT WAS A BOY, he began redrawing the political cartoons he saw in his father's newspaper, *Appeal to Reason*. This led to his penchant for drawing caricatures. One day, Walt drew impressions of the patrons at Bert Hudson's barbershop in Kansas City. The barber liked them so much he asked Walt to draw a new caricature every week in exchange for haircuts. At the age of nine, to amuse his sister Ruth when she became ill with measles, Walt created a series of drawings that, when flipped, seemed to move. At this very young age, Walt was making his first attempts at animation. He later took art classes at the Kansas City Art Institute and enjoyed them more than his regular schoolwork.

At McKinley High School in Chicago, Walt joined the staff of *The Voice*, the school periodical, as an artist. There, he worked long hours creating his cartoons and would never show anyone what he was working on until he completed it. He also began assembling a gag file, a reference of ideas for personal use. On one occasion Walt tried out a few of his best jokes on his father, as Elias listened on. Walt remembered that after two days had passed, a straight-faced Elias said to him, "You know, I've been thinking about that joke you told me, Walter. It's funny, very funny."

TOP Sketch for *The Voice* drawn by Walt, c. 1918; printed ink on paper

BOTTOM Pages from *The Voice* school magazine, 1918; printed ink on paper

OPPOSITE *The Voice* school magazine, 1918; printed ink on paper

The Voice

McKinley High School

Chicago, Illinois

June, 1918

THE VOICE

Tuesday evening, April 23, the Seniors gave a "Hard Time" prom, in our gym,—and, did we have a good time! Let me tell you about it: All the Seniors came dressed up in their "old clothes" to represent the hard times that are now prevailing, and as one stepped into the gym, the most comical and grotesque scenes met his eye! For instance, George Boller wore a black top coat somewhat like a frock, with grey trousers so short that some one suggested that he "make a party on his trousers and invite his shoes up." Miss Mack certainly looked like "hard times" in every sense of the word, with an old patched velvet dress on and a hat which slightly suggested the year 1700. The attire of the Steiner sisters provided much amusement. I should not say we are exactly inquisitive, Ruth, but didn't you wear one black stocking and one red?

The dancing was superb. Of course, how could it be otherwise when Baselah Cristol was one of the musicians? Even Mr. Payne danced with—?

In the midst of the enjoyment some one said something about home-made fudge and instantly all the girls began to pass the fudge out. Now, I'll tell you a little secret: The boys who, fortunately, are provided with that wonderful quality called "tact," sweetly went up to the girls with such phrases as "Oh, I never eat fudge, but of course, when you make it, why—er——" and "I could eat your fudge forever." Now, three guesses as to who got the most fudge.

While the "fudge feastin'" was going on we were entertained with a dancing demonstration by Sophie Fink and Louis Golan.

After this there were many games and more dancing until Miss Mack decided that we "trot off" home, so she rang the bell and we all very reluctantly left the gym where the graduating class of '18 had so successfully given their first "war-time prom." (which will not by far be their last).

Help! We are stranded on the bottom of page 78.

Twenty-eight

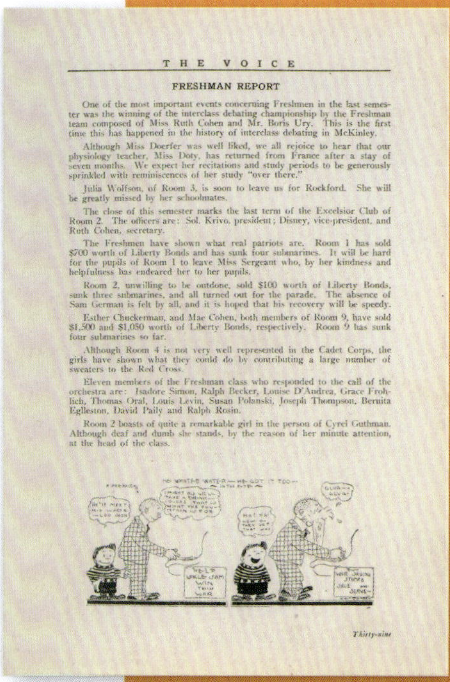

THE VOICE

FRESHMAN REPORT

One of the most important events concerning Freshmen in the last semester was the winning of the interclass debating championship by the Freshman team composed of Miss Ruth Cohen and Mr. Boris Ury. This is the first time this has happened in the history of interclass debating in McKinley.

Although Miss Doerfer was well liked, we all rejoice to hear that our physiology teacher, Miss Doty, has returned from France after a stay of seven months. We expect her recitations and study periods to be generously sprinkled with reminiscences of her study "over there."

Julia Wolfson, of Room 3, is soon to leave us for Rockford. She will be greatly missed by her schoolmates.

The close of this semester marks the last term of the Excelsior Club of Room 2. The officers are: Sol. Krivo, president; Disney, vice-president, and Ruth Cohen, secretary.

The Freshmen have shown what real patriots are. Room 1 has sold $700 worth of Liberty Bonds and has sunk four submarines. It will be hard for the pupils of Room 1 to leave Miss Sergeant who, by her kindness and helpfulness has endeared her to her pupils.

Room 2, unwilling to be outdone, sold $100 worth of Liberty Bonds, sunk three submarines, and all turned out for the parade. The absence of Sam German is felt by all, and it is hoped that his recovery will be speedy.

Esther Chuckerman, and Mae Cohen, both members of Room 9, have sold $1,500 and $1,050 worth of Liberty Bonds, respectively. Room 9 has sunk four submarines so far.

Although Room 4 is not very well represented in the Cadet Corps, the girls have shown what they could do by contributing a large number of sweaters to the Red Cross.

Eleven members of the Freshman class who responded to the call of the orchestra are: Isadore Simon, Ralph Becker, Louise D'Andrea, Grace Frohlich, Thomas Oral, Louis Levin, Susan Polanski, Joseph Thompson, Bernita Eggleston, David Paily and Ralph Rosin.

Room 2 boasts of quite a remarkable girl in the person of Cyrel Guthman. Although deaf and dumb she stands, by the reason of her minute attention, at the head of the class.

Thirty-nine

WALT'S
1918 PASSPORT

WHEN WORLD WAR I BEGAN, and his older brothers joined the military, Walt was determined to serve as well. At sixteen, he was too young for the Armed Forces, but he found the American Red Cross ambulance corps would take seventeen-year-old volunteers, as long as his parents approved. His mother preferred to know where he was going than to have him run off. He forged the document his mother signed—inflating his age by a year—allowing him to join the cause and travel to France. "My mother made this affidavit out that her son Walter Elias Disney was born December 5, 1901, and this and that and she gave permission and ... signed it. She put it down and she'd ... no more turned her back then I picked up the pen and from the '1' I made a '0.' " Walt's official 1918 passport listed his birthday as December 5, 1900.

During training from the Yellow Cab Company on how to repair motors, and disassemble and reassemble cars, an influenza epidemic struck the camp. Walt grew so ill he was sent home to be cared for by his parents. To his dismay, by the time he had recovered, his unit had already sailed for France. He returned to auxiliary service, and a week later, on November 11, 1918, an armistice calling for the ceasefire between the Allies and Germany was signed. Even though this was an exciting time in the United States, Walt felt as if he had missed the call to action and was eager to continue to France to do his part. One week after the ceasefire, the Red Cross arranged to send fifty members of his company to France to assist occupation forces. Walt's name was the last to be called, and on November 18 he embarked for France on an old rusty cattle ship, the *Vaubin*.

WALT'S
MEMENTOS OF RED CROSS SERVICE

THIS BAG OF WWI TREASURES was found by Walt's grandson, Walter Miller. "When I was twelve or thirteen years old, my Granny Lilly gifted me a valet box that belonged to my grandpa. Underneath the top shelf of this box ... there was a small weathered old bag that had many small items in it that appeared to be full of mementos from the time he spent in France with the Red Cross." Inside the bag were an assortment of coins from Brazil, France, French Indochina, Germany, Italy, the Philippines, the UK, and Tunisia; some U.S. military buttons; a Prussian Iron Cross; a French Rooster lighter; a small photo book with scenes from Paris; a collection of Red Cross pins; and more.

Walt's daughter Diane remembers that as a child she would open her father's valet box to view its contents, but she never had looked beneath the top shelf. "I was not at all aware [that] this grubby little bag of dad's was collected during this very important experience, during his seventeenth year, and kept all his life."

OPPOSITE TOP Walt's passport, 1918; leather cover, handwritten and printed ink on paper, and photograph

OPPOSITE BOTTOM Collection of Walt's World War I–era memorabilia, including coins, buttons, pins, a photo mini-book, ribbons, etc., c. 1917

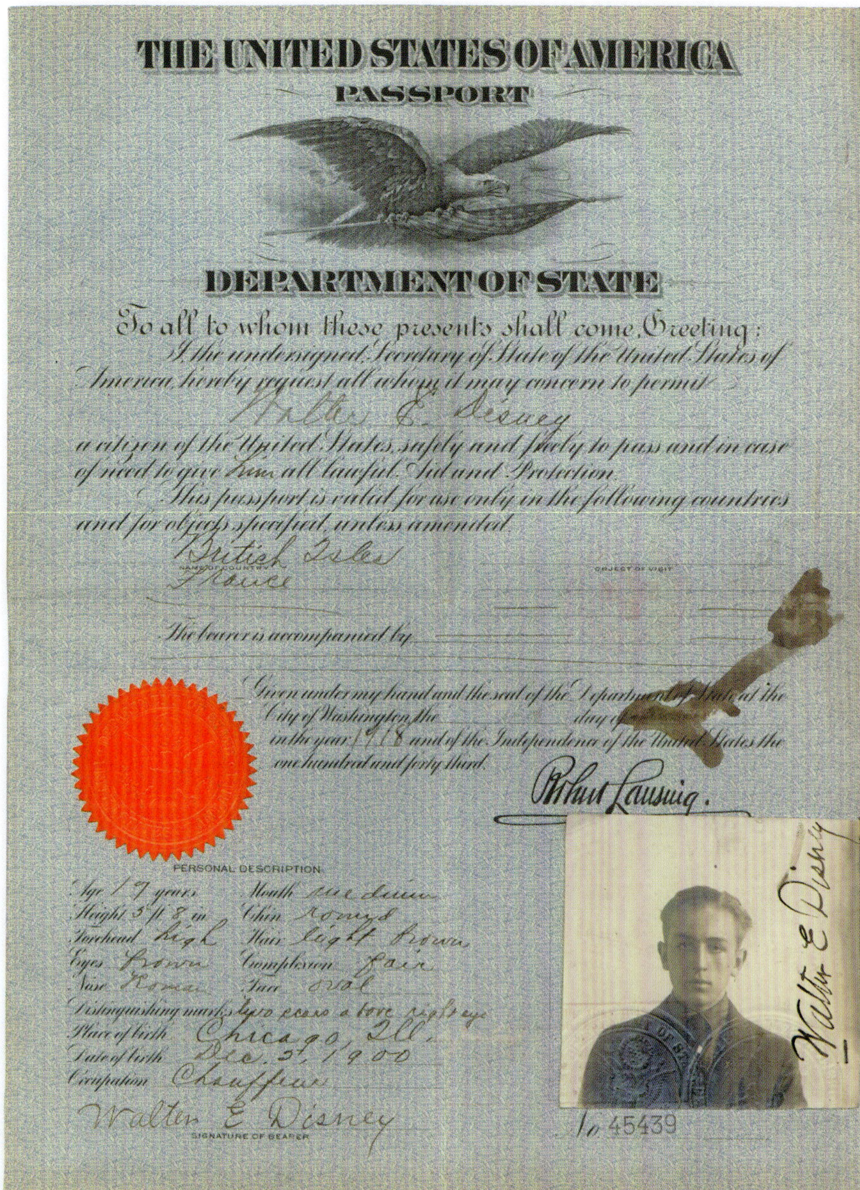
THE UNITED STATES OF AMERICA

PASSPORT

DEPARTMENT OF STATE

To all to whom these presents shall come, Greeting:

I, the undersigned, Secretary of State of the United States of America, hereby request all whom it may concern to permit Walter E. Disney a citizen of the United States, safely and freely to pass and in case of need to give him all lawful Aid and Protection.

This passport is valid for use only in the following countries and for objects specified, unless amended.

British Isles

France

OBJECT OF VISIT

The bearer is accompanied by

Given under my hand and the seal of the Department of State at the City of Washington, the day of in the year 1918 and of the Independence of the United States the one hundred and forty third.

Robert Lansing.

PERSONAL DESCRIPTION.

Age 17 years Mouth medium

Height 5 ft 8 in Chin round

Forehead high Hair light brown

Eyes brown Complexion fair

Nose Roman Face oval

Distinguishing marks [illegible]

Place of birth Chicago, Ill.

Date of birth Dec. 5th 1900

Occupation Chauffeur

Walter E. Disney

SIGNATURE OF BEARER

No 45439

LAUGH-O-GRAM FILMS

UNIVERSAL CAMERA

AFTER WALT RETURNED FROM FRANCE, he eventually arrived in Kansas City eager to make his start as a professional artist. His first job was with the Pesmen-Rubin Commercial Art Studio, where he became fast friends with Ub Iwerks. After working at a film company where he learned stop-motion animation, and a stint teaching students how to create cartoons, Walt's determination to make animated films was realized when on May 23, 1922, he incorporated his new studio, Laugh-O-gram Films, thanks to $15,000 he received from local investors. Walt persuaded Ub Iwerks to leave his job and they hired five young animators, including their first female artist, Aletha Reynolds.

Always experimenting, he bought a Universal (Burke & James) 35mm hand-crank motion picture camera and tripod, like the one pictured above, for three hundred dollars. On the weekends he would drive through downtown Kansas City filming the world around him. He even filmed home movies of babies for extra cash. Walt then struck a deal with a non-theatrical distribution company, Pictorial Clubs—they sent Walt a check for one hundred dollars and a note promising $11,000 for six cartoons. The Laugh-O-gram studio would end up producing fairy tale films such as *Little Red Riding Hood*, *Goldilocks and the Three Bears*, *Cinderella*, and more. Ever the renaissance man, Walt produced some of the animation, operated the camera, and even performed tasks like washing celluloid sheets so they could be reused.

LAUGH-O-GRAM FILMS
FILES FOR BANKRUPTCY

IN LATE JULY 1923, Walt Disney's Laugh-O-gram Films studio was headed for bankruptcy. As salary checks grew thinner, Walt's staff began to find steady jobs elsewhere. Even Ub Iwerks left the company and returned to his previous job. With finances dwindling, Walt stayed with Ub for a couple of weeks, before eventually sleeping in the Laugh-O-gram offices, where his rent had been paid in advance. He ate on credit at the cafe downstairs, where his bill eventually totaled sixty dollars—or, in today's dollars, approximately seven hundred and fifty dollars. Without proper lodging, Walt would make weekly journeys to the local railroad station to buy time in a warm tub, a towel, and a bar of soap for a dime.

As bankruptcy proceedings were being finalized, Walt purchased a one-way ticket on the *California Limited* to Hollywood. With just forty dollars in his pocket, an old suitcase, and some drawing materials, Walt left Kansas City behind to embark upon a new path in Hollywood. When he arrived, he was determined and optimistic. "Maybe I was just naïve, but I never had the feeling I couldn't get a job. I'd be disillusioned and upset when I couldn't get what I wanted. But this business of being worried about something—I never had that," shared Walt. "I never felt sorry for myself."

"I think it's important to have a good hard failure when you're young."

—WALT

TOP Walt's stationery design, c. 1922

BOTTOM Walt at a Laugh-O-gram studio drawing board, c. 1922

OPPOSITE TOP Universal camera; metal, wood, and leather

OPPOSITE BOTTOM Walt and Fred Harman standing behind a Universal camera, 1922

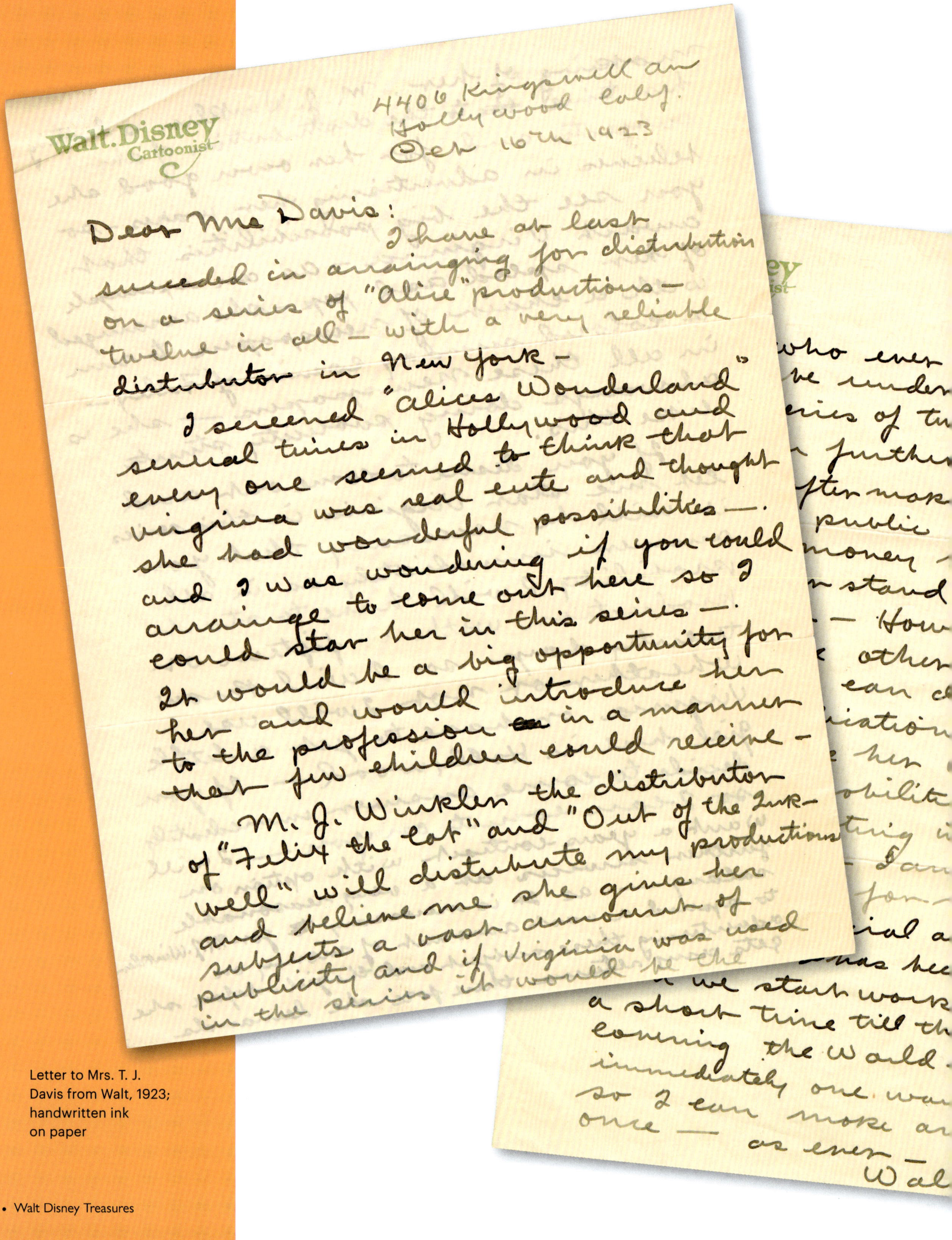
Walt. Disney
Cartoonist

4406 Kingswell Av
Hollywood Calif.
Oct 16th 1923

Dear Mrs Davis:

I have at last succeded in arrainging for distribution on a series of "Alice" productions — twelve in all — with a very reliable distributor in New York —

I screened "Alices Wonderland" several times in Hollywood and every one seemed to think that Virginia was real cute and thought she had wonderful possibilites —. and I was wondering if you could arrainge to come out here so I could star her in this series —. It would be a big opportunity for her and would introduce her to the profession in a manner that few children could receive —

M. J. Winkler the distributor of "Felix the Cat" and "Out of the Inkwell" will distribute my productions and believe me she gives her subjects a vast amount of publicity and if Virginia was used in the series it would be the

Letter to Mrs. T. J. Davis from Walt, 1923; handwritten ink on paper

WALT'S

LETTER TO MRS. T. J. DAVIS

WALT TRAVELED TO HOLLYWOOD IN 1923 with one last film project, a pilot cartoon short, *Alice's Wonderland* (1923), featuring a live-action girl Alice in an animated Cartoonland, performed by Virginia Davis. Walt contacted one of the biggest cartoon distributors of the day, Margaret J. Winkler of Winkler Pictures about the film. On October 16, 1923, Walt and Roy O. Disney established the Disney Brothers Cartoon Studio when they signed a contract with Winkler for distribution of an initial series of Alice Comedies short films. She specified in her original telegram that Alice had to be played by the same little girl in the unfinished pilot reel. On that same day, Walt wrote a letter to Virginia Davis's mother.

"When I was four a letter came from California," Virginia Davis remembered. "There were two different things in there ... that ... this *Alice's Wonderland* was okay'd and he had gotten a distributor—M. J. Winkler as a matter of fact. He thought that would be terrific for me and he proceeded to do a great selling job in the letter to my mother."

Davis's father agreed to move his family to California and Walt promised to pay his young star well, making Virginia the studio's highest paid employee. Successfully selling the Alice Comedies to Winkler and Hollywood to the Davis family emboldened Walt with confidence that if he truly believed in a product or an idea, he could sell it to just about anyone.

ALICE
THE
PEACEMAKER
To Diane and Ron:
My very best wishes always to you both and to your family!
Love
Virginia Davis
"Alice"
A WALT DISNEY COMIC
M.J. WINKLER
DISTRIBUTOR, N.Y.
WINKLER PICTURES
Ritchey
MP3521

ALICE THE PEACEMAKER (1924)

FILM POSTER

CLEVERLY ESTABLISHING HERSELF in the industry as "M. J. Winkler," Margaret Winkler would become the first female member of the Motion Picture Producers Guild. Winkler worked at the Warner Bros. studio as a secretary to Harry Warner at age eighteen. Warner recognized her aptitude for business and suggested Winkler handle the distribution of Max Fleischer's Out of the Inkwell series.

By the time she was twenty-six, she started her own company, M. J. Winkler Productions, to produce and distribute animated cartoons. Winkler revitalized the character and put Felix the Cat on the map.

Acceptance was not always forthcoming from her male peers. When asked if people were surprised her company was owned by a woman, she responded that they were "sometimes scared, but they got over it."

Margaret J. Winkler was the only female leader in the male-dominated world of movie distribution at the time. At the helm of Winkler Productions, she established animation as a sustainable division of the entertainment industry and played a key role in the start of what we know today as The Walt Disney Company.

LEFT Margaret Winkler, c. 1923

OPPOSITE *Alice the Peacemaker* (1924) poster signed by Virginia Davis; handwritten and printed ink on paper

"More than any other medium, the motion picture is being challenged to meet the greatly enlarged opportunities and responsibilities of modern showmanship."

—WALT

PATHÉ STUDIO CAMERA

AT THE START of the Disney Brothers Cartoon Studio in 1923, Walt wrote, directed, and drew all the shorts, while Roy managed the books and operated their secondhand Pathé studio camera. Two women were eventually hired to ink and paint the celluloids. The first reel for the Alice Comedies was finished on schedule and delivered the day after Christmas 1923. With encouragement from Winkler, Walt concentrated his efforts on adding more gags into each subsequent Alice Comedy short. For ten dollars a month, he rented a vacant lot at Hollywood Boulevard and Rodney Drive, where he could photograph live-action with Virginia Davis and neighborhood kids. Alice's dog was portrayed by a German Shepherd named Peggy, who was owned by Walt's uncle, Robert Disney.

The Pathé camera was a workhorse camera of the film industry during the 1920s. Pathé Freres was the leader in motion picture technology and developed the Pathé camera in 1908. It was widely distributed from the 1910s through the 1920s. A lightweight camera with a wooden exterior made to be easily transportable, the Pathé had a single-frame crank capability for special effects use or the capture of animation. It remained the industry standard for silent films in Hollywood until the introduction of the Bell & Howell all-metal cameras heading into the 1920s.

BELL & HOWELL CAMERA

EARLY ALICE COMEDY SHORTS were primarily filmed with a Pathé camera. With the success of the Alice Comedies, the Disney brothers were able to rent a Bell & Howell camera to film the live-action scenes. The Pathé camera was relegated to filming the animation for the series.

The Bell & Howell Model 2709 Standard Cinemachinery was a hand-crank camera produced from 1912 through 1958. This camera had a reputation for precision, durability, and reliability that made it a favorite of Charlie Chaplin—one of Walt's favorite silent film actors.

This 2709 dominated the market that was long held by Pathé Studios and by 1919, it is estimated that all equipment used to make movies in Hollywood was manufactured by Bell & Howell. The 2709 model was used to film such silent film classics as *Ben-Hur: A Tale of the Christ* (1925) and Charlie Chaplin's *The Gold Rush* (1925).

LEFT Pathé camera, c. 1920; metal and wood

RIGHT Bell & Howell camera and tripod, c. 1920; metal and wood

COUNTRY OF ORIGIN U.S.A.

33092

OSWALD THE LUCKY RABBIT

ANIMATION SKETCHES AND POSTER

AS THE ALICE COMEDIES CAME TO AN END, Universal Pictures and studio head Carl Laemmle were interested in developing a cartoon series starring a rabbit character. Universal brainstormed with distributor Charles Mintz about who would be the best to bring the rabbit to the screen. Margaret Winkler—original distributor for the Disney Brothers Cartoon Studio and Mintz's wife—suggested that Walt might be the best person to tackle the series. Universal approved the Disney studio's initial sketches and Mintz told Walt the good news. This all-new character would be christened Oswald the Lucky Rabbit.

Walt, Ub Iwerks, and the Disney studio staff collaborated to create an appealing animated series that was lauded by the media of the era. By the end of 1927, Walt had hired more artists and grew his staff to twenty-two. Iwerks and his fellow animators began turning out an Oswald cartoon every two weeks.

In February 1928, the Oswald contract was nearing its completion. Walt treated his wife Lillian to a train trip to New York for a renewal negotiation with Mintz and Universal. During the negotiations, Walt discovered a tough reality: even though his rising studio had animated and established the character, Oswald was owned by Universal. He did not have the rights to the character he had created. Disheartened by the news, Walt vowed to never again work for someone else.

LEFT Ub Iwerks, animation drawings for *Rival Romeos* (1928); graphite on paper

OPPOSITE "I'm Oswald, the Lucky Rabbit" poster, c. 1927; printed ink on paper

TELEGRAM NOTING THE
LOSS OF OSWALD THE LUCKY RABBIT

AFTER WALT AND ROY LEARNED they had no rights to Oswald the Lucky Rabbit—Walt's first venture into fully animated cartoons—they were determined to create a new series to keep their business afloat.

Walt later recalled, "Before coming home [from New York], I tried to create another character ... and sell the idea to some distributor before I left, on the strength of the work that I had done on Oswald. I couldn't find anyone who was interested in the idea, so again I thought the best thing to do was make a picture. However, it was quite a problem to decide what to use. [Cartoon producers] had used cats, dogs, rabbits. About the only thing they hadn't featured was the mouse."

In his 1947 recorded remarks for the radio program *University of the Air,* Walt called Mickey Mouse "a symbol of independence," both financially and creatively. Mickey was, in a sense, born out of necessity for the Disney brothers: in 1928, the year of Mickey's debut, the Disneys' finances and creative prospects were at a low point. The near-immediate success of this simple and unassuming character gave Walt and Roy the means to expand their modest cartoon studio and led to new opportunities in animation and beyond.

Famously, Walt's wife, Lillian, talked him out of naming the mouse "Mortimer" and they eventually settled on Mickey. As Walt himself said, "Well, I like Mickey ... you feel you can be friendly with anyone named Mickey." Throughout the decade that followed, Mickey became one of the world's most recognizable and beloved movie stars and pop culture icons.

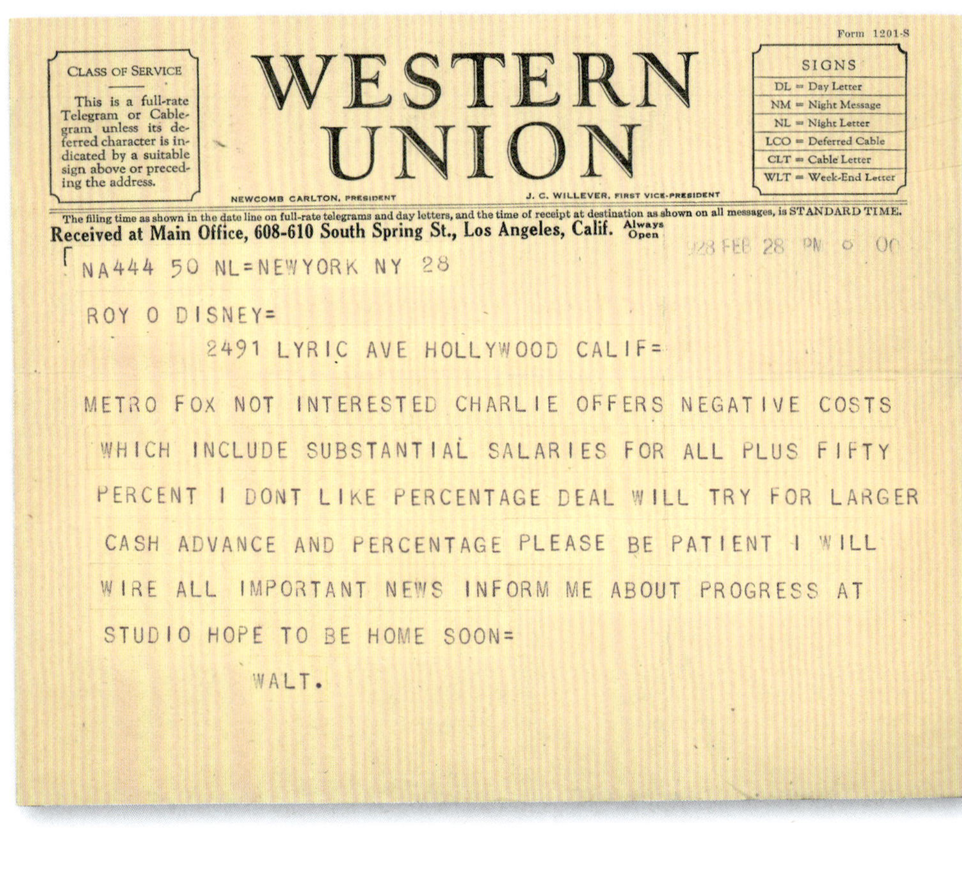

Form 1201-S

CLASS OF SERVICE
This is a full-rate Telegram or Cablegram unless its deferred character is indicated by a suitable sign above or preceding the address.

WESTERN UNION

NEWCOMB CARLTON, PRESIDENT J. C. WILLEVER, FIRST VICE-PRESIDENT

SIGNS
DL = Day Letter
NM = Night Message
NL = Night Letter
LCO = Deferred Cable
CLT = Cable Letter
WLT = Week-End Letter

The filing time as shown in the date line on full-rate telegrams and day letters, and the time of receipt at destination as shown on all messages, is STANDARD TIME.
Received at Main Office, 608-610 South Spring St., Los Angeles, Calif. Always Open

1928 FEB 28 PM 9 00

NA444 50 NL=NEWYORK NY 28

ROY O DISNEY=
2491 LYRIC AVE HOLLYWOOD CALIF=

METRO FOX NOT INTERESTED CHARLIE OFFERS NEGATIVE COSTS WHICH INCLUDE SUBSTANTIAL SALARIES FOR ALL PLUS FIFTY PERCENT I DONT LIKE PERCENTAGE DEAL WILL TRY FOR LARGER CASH ADVANCE AND PERCENTAGE PLEASE BE PATIENT I WILL WIRE ALL IMPORTANT NEWS INFORM ME ABOUT PROGRESS AT STUDIO HOPE TO BE HOME SOON=

WALT.

RIGHT Telegram to Roy from Walt, February 28, 1928; printed ink on paper

OPPOSITE Letter to Roy from Walt, March 7, 1928; handwritten ink on paper

New York
Mar 7th

Dear Roy —

Well we are still hanging
around this Hell Hole waiting for
something to happen — before
you get this letter I hope you
will have had a wire containing
good news — I can't rush things
any faster — just have to do
the best I can BUT I WILL
FIGHT IT OUT ON THIS LINE IF
IT TAKES ALL SUMMER and all
our jack — It sure looks
like a fight to a finish — Charlie
is very determined to get absolute
controll of everything and will
do everything in his power to gain
his end — But unknown to
him we have a stronger power
than he on our side

Monday Universal told me
they would talk to Charlie &
let me hear from them afterwards
I hardly expected to hear from them
tuesday but stuck around close
waiting for a call — NO WORD —
I didn't want to pester them so
I waited all day today and still
no word so this P.M. at 5 o'clock

EARLIEST KNOWN DRAWING OF **MICKEY MOUSE AND MINNIE MOUSE**

IN THE EARLY 1990s, Bill Cottrell, Walt's brother-in-law and President of Retlaw Enterprises, a private corporation managed by Walt's family, told Diane there was "something special" in the Retlaw vault. When she looked in the vault, she found this rough drawing along with a "clean-up" drawing. The drawing has been authenticated as the earliest known drawing of Mickey Mouse and Minnie Mouse in existence.

Authorship of the individual drawings has never been definitively established. Ub Iwerks certainly had a hand in them, but Walt and possibly animator Les Clark also contributed. You can see the decision-making process in these rough animation sketches as Walt, Ub, and Les explored and developed the character designs. This drawing also helps to confirm that Mickey Mouse and Minnie Mouse were created at the same time, reinforced by their on-screen debut in *Steamboat Willie* (1928).

Mickey Mouse's earliest design was similar to that of Oswald the Lucky Rabbit. Though Mickey had a different nose, tail, and ears, one can still see the similarities between the two characters that Walt and Ub brought to life.

Earliest known drawings of Mickey Mouse and Minnie Mouse, 1928; graphite and colored pencil on paper

THE SKELETON DANCE (1929)

BACKGROUND PAINTING

MICKEY MOUSE WAS A HUGE SUCCESS for Walt, but he knew that it was just the start of what he could do. With the ease that came with extra income from the success of *Steamboat Willie* (1928), Walt was able to consider other types of animation and artistry.

This painting is a background from one of Walt's next projects, an animation series that featured music instead of characters as the focus. Composer Carl Stalling pitched Walt on an idea for musical shorts with a different cast of characters. Walt approved and the Silly Symphony series was born. Stalling had the idea for a short about dancing skeletons that originated from his youth and Walt thought it would work great for this new direction. Production began on this new skeleton short in early 1929, just mere months after Mickey's November 1928 premiere in *Steamboat Willie*.

The Skeleton Dance opens at the "bewitching hour" with lightning strikes, a hooting owl, two fighting cats, and a descending spider. After the spooky mood is set, four skeletons rise from the graveyard to frolic in the moonlight. The skeletons then perform a traditional vaudeville routine as a choreographed dance for the audience, all set to Stalling's memorable score.

THE CREATION OF MICKEY MOUSE

SPECIAL ACADEMY AWARD®

MICKEY MOUSE DEBUTED in the trailblazing cartoon *Steamboat Willie* (1928), the first animated cartoon to feature synchronized sound. By the 1930s, at the height of his early popularity, Mickey was starring in more than a dozen cartoons each year. In 1948, Walt commented, "[Mickey] has appeared in more pictures than any flesh and blood star."

At the fifth annual Academy Awards ceremony held on November 18, 1932, Walt Disney was the man of the hour. The Academy of Motion Picture Arts and Sciences celebrated Mickey's four-year anniversary with an honorary special award for the "Creation of Mickey Mouse." This award established Mickey Mouse as one of the most important cartoon characters ever created.

This night also introduced the Short Subject (Cartoon) category, and brought Walt his first competitive Academy Award, for the Silly Symphony short, *Flowers and Trees* (winning against another Disney cartoon, *Mickey's Orphans*).

According to the conservators at The Walt Disney Family Museum, the Mickey Mouse award was originally plated in matte, light gold. In the early 1990s, the statue was sent to the Academy for their complimentary replating services and was returned replated in the current standard Academy Award 24-karat gold.

LEFT Honorary Academy Award for the creation of Mickey Mouse, 1932; cast metal on wood base

OPPOSITE Disney Studio Artist, background painting for *The Skeleton Dance* (1929); watercolor and ink on paper

BELOW U.S. Navy white service hat signed by members of The Walt Disney Studios, including Walt, c. 1940s; applied ink and graphite on cotton drill

OPPOSITE Wolfgang Reitherman and Retta Scott, *B-1st* children's book mock-up, 1941; graphite, colored pencil, and paint on paper

DISNEY STUDIO EMPLOYEE-SIGNED
U.S. NAVY SERVICE HAT

LIKE MOST AMERICANS, Walt was at home on the morning of Sunday, December 7, 1941, when the radio broadcast the news about the attack on Pearl Harbor. Walt recalled when the Disney Studios manager called and said, "Walt, the Army is moving in on us ... they came up and said they wanted to move in." The Studios manager told the Army that he would have to call Walt, and they responded, "Call him, but we're moving in anyway."

Walt Disney was eager to serve his country once again. One of the few Hollywood film studios under military occupation, The Walt Disney Studios enthusiastically responded to the call to arms, devoting more than 90 percent of its wartime output to producing training, propaganda, entertainment, and educational films, as well as designing insignia and print media.

One of Walt's pressing concerns was losing his studio artists to military service. Several of them received deferments to remain on war-related film projects, but many Disney personnel donned uniforms. This Navy service hat was signed by studio employees and Walt Disney back on the home front showing support for their service members.

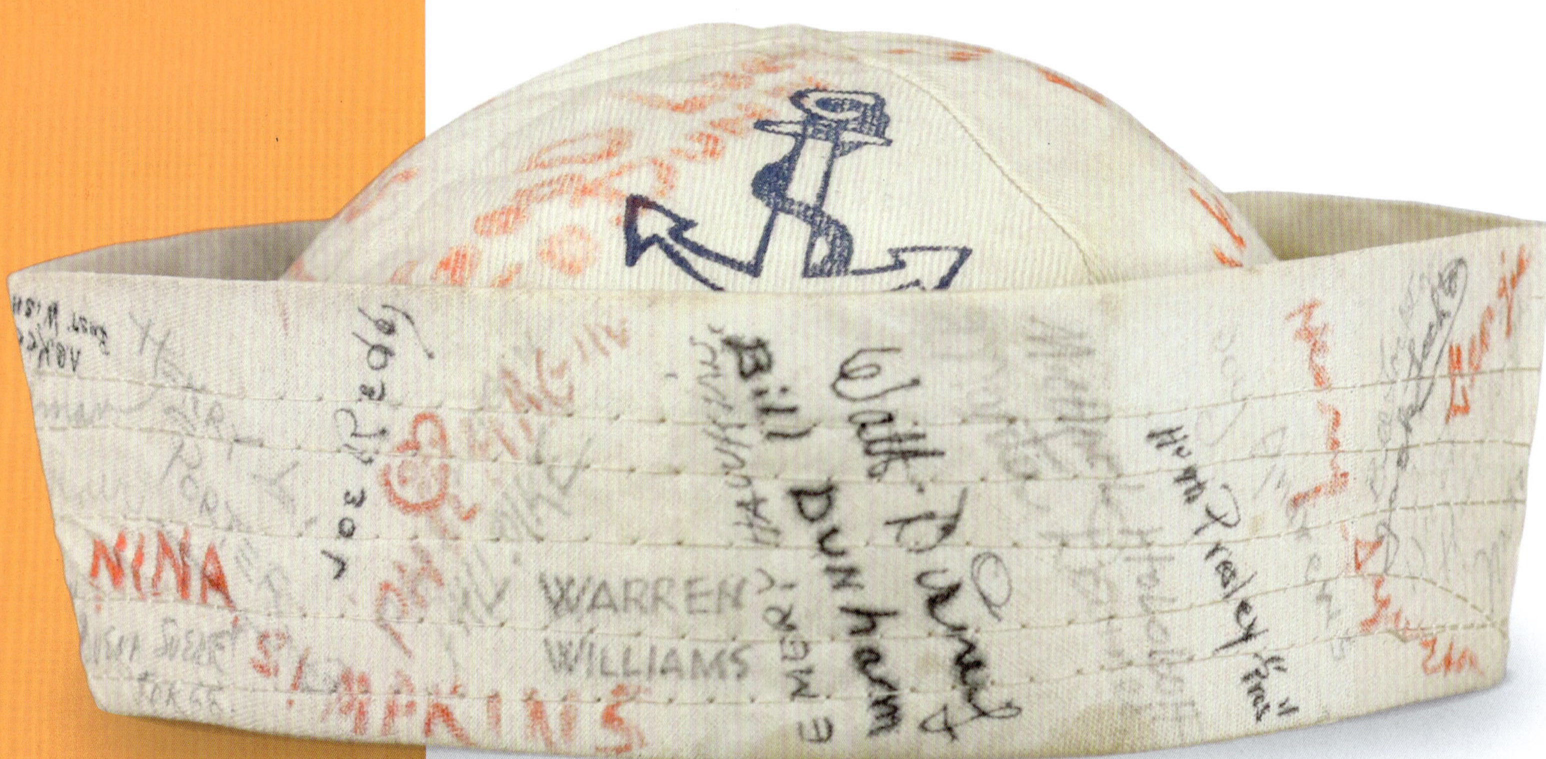

DISNEY ANIMATORS

CHILDREN'S BOOK MOCK-UP

THREE MONTHS BEFORE THE ATTACK ON PEARL HARBOR, Retta Scott, Disney's first female animator, and Woolie Reitherman, a key studio animator, collaborated on a mock-up of a children's book called *B-1st* as an outside project. Reitherman joined the U.S. Armed Forces as a pilot after the attack on Pearl Harbor, and the book project sat unfinished.

B-1st is a story about a fictitious U.S. Army pursuit plane that must be designed and tested in thirty days, but a saboteur sneaks in and cracks one of the pistons during assembly. B-1st's initial test flight goes off without a hitch, but then realizes he has a piston problem and stubbornly flies to a high altitude anyway, quickly setting altitude and speed records. But when the piston suddenly pops out through the engine compartment, he spins out of control, crashing to the ground. A spark of life is found in one of B-1st's spark plugs, and he is quickly repaired before the thirty-day deadline arrives. He then roars off into the sky to "B-1st" in America's defense.

The book would go unpublished for seventy-five years, until Disney historian Didier Ghez discovered the yellowing manuscript in 2015 and the book was finally published in 2016, with the original anthropomorphic aircraft art.

"Walt always challenged new horizons and challenged himself and his staff."

—RON MILLER, *WALT'S SON-IN-LAW*

TREASURE ISLAND (1950)

WALT'S PIECE OF EIGHT PROP

THIS "PIECE OF EIGHT" IS A PROP from the Disney live-action film *Treasure Island* (1950). Made from cast metal, the Disney prop coins made up the bulk of treasure taken by Long John Silver as he rows away at the end of the film. Also known as Spanish dollars, pieces of eight were so named because they were worth eight *reals*, the base unit of Spain's colonial currency. Pieces of eight circulated widely in the Western Hemisphere starting in the fifteenth century and went on to form the basis of numerous national currencies, including the U.S. dollar.

From early in his career to the early 1940s, Walt had undoubtedly innovated within animated cartoons—and live-action to a lesser degree. Walt had wanted to become a live-action filmmaker when he first arrived in Hollywood and with *Treasure Island*, he finally achieved this dream. This film opened a new chapter for Walt Disney Productions and was an opportunity for Walt to experiment with a form of filmmaking that had long intrigued him. As one animator said, "We realized that as soon as Walt rode on a camera crane, we were going to lose him."

In many ways, *Treasure Island* helped lay the foundation for Walt's later successes. It served as an inspiration for the artists working on the *Pirates of the Caribbean* attraction for Disneyland Park, and even later for the live-action films made by the studio based on the iconic attraction. It could be said that *Treasure Island* marked the beginning of a swashbuckling new era of adventure and expansion for Walt and his eponymous company.

RIGHT Piece of Eight prop from *Treasure Island* (1950), 1949; cast metal

OPPOSITE Mitchell CinemaScope underwater camera used for *20,000 Leagues Under the Sea* (1954); metal and plastic

MITCHELL CINEMASCOPE
UNDERWATER CAMERA

THE FILMING OF *20,000 LEAGUES UNDER THE SEA* (1954) required special equipment for underwater scenes: the Mitchell 35mm High Speed CinemaScope Camera. The camera had special housing so it could easily maneuver underwater. It was operated by underwater photographer Till Gabbani. The cameraman wrote for the *American Cinematographer* in 1954, "THIRTY FEET underwater in the Caribbean, off Nassau, Bahamas, some eighty motion picture artists and technicians wearing safety diving gear recently completed what unquestionably was the most challenging assignment ever faced by a Hollywood motion picture troupe. Here on the ocean floor was filmed in Eastman Color with a CinemaScope lens the fabulous underwater sequences for Walt Disney's version of Jules Verne's '20,000 Leagues Under the Sea.'"

The Mitchell camera was used for stationary shots underwater utilizing a heavy metal tripod. Camera assistants, prop handlers, and grips were all required to be underwater along with the camera operator and the equipment. Studio lights could not be used in the underwater scenes, so the crew utilized natural sunlight to light their scenes, making the shooting even more complex.

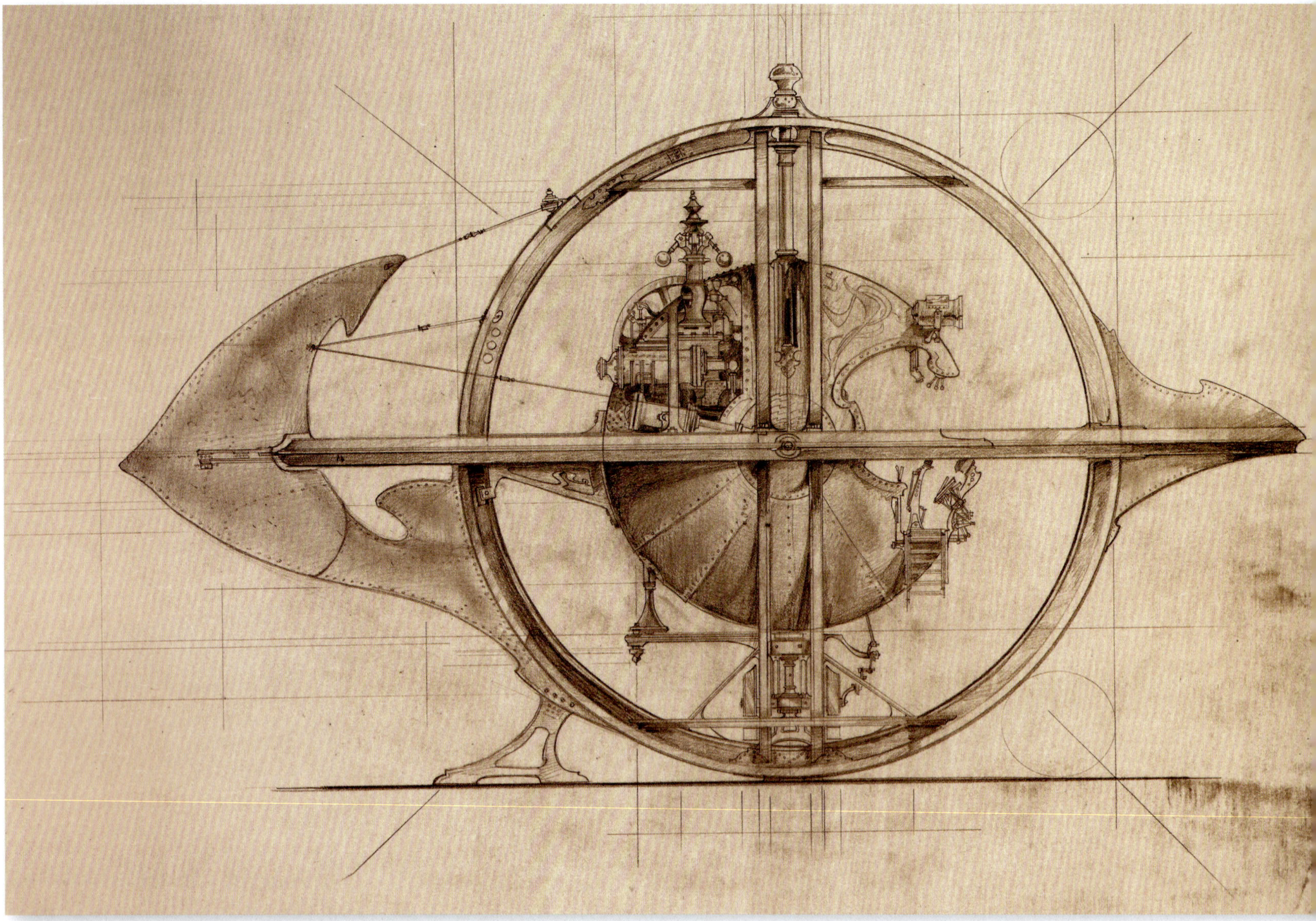

20,000 LEAGUES UNDER THE SEA (1954)

HARPER GOFF *NAUTILUS* CONCEPT AND SCRAPBOOK

WALT HAD BEEN A LONGTIME FAN of Jules Verne's classic 1870 novel, *20,000 Leagues Under the Sea*, but wasn't sure what he wanted to do with it. Initially, Walt asked artist Harper Goff to create a pitch for a *True-Life Adventures* documentary inspired by Verne's novel. While Walt was away on a trip to London, Goff instead came up with the idea for a live-action feature version of the book and created storyboards for it. When he returned, Walt was upset that Goff had not followed his directions, but the more he studied Goff's storyboards, the more he liked them.

Goff oversaw the visual design of the film, including the exterior design of the *Nautilus*, the centerpiece of the film where most of the action takes place. He studied the novel in detail, aiming to interpret Jules Verne's descriptions in a way that would be faithful to the original book, but also be visually exciting on film.

In time, *20,000 Leagues Under the Sea* (1954) wound up being the most expensive film The Walt Disney Studios had made to date. The final budget put it among the five most expensive movies ever produced at that time. But the effort and investment paid off: it was a critical and commercial success. Disney made back more than the initial investment in the production, and it went on to win two Academy Awards® for Art Direction (Color) and Special Effects.

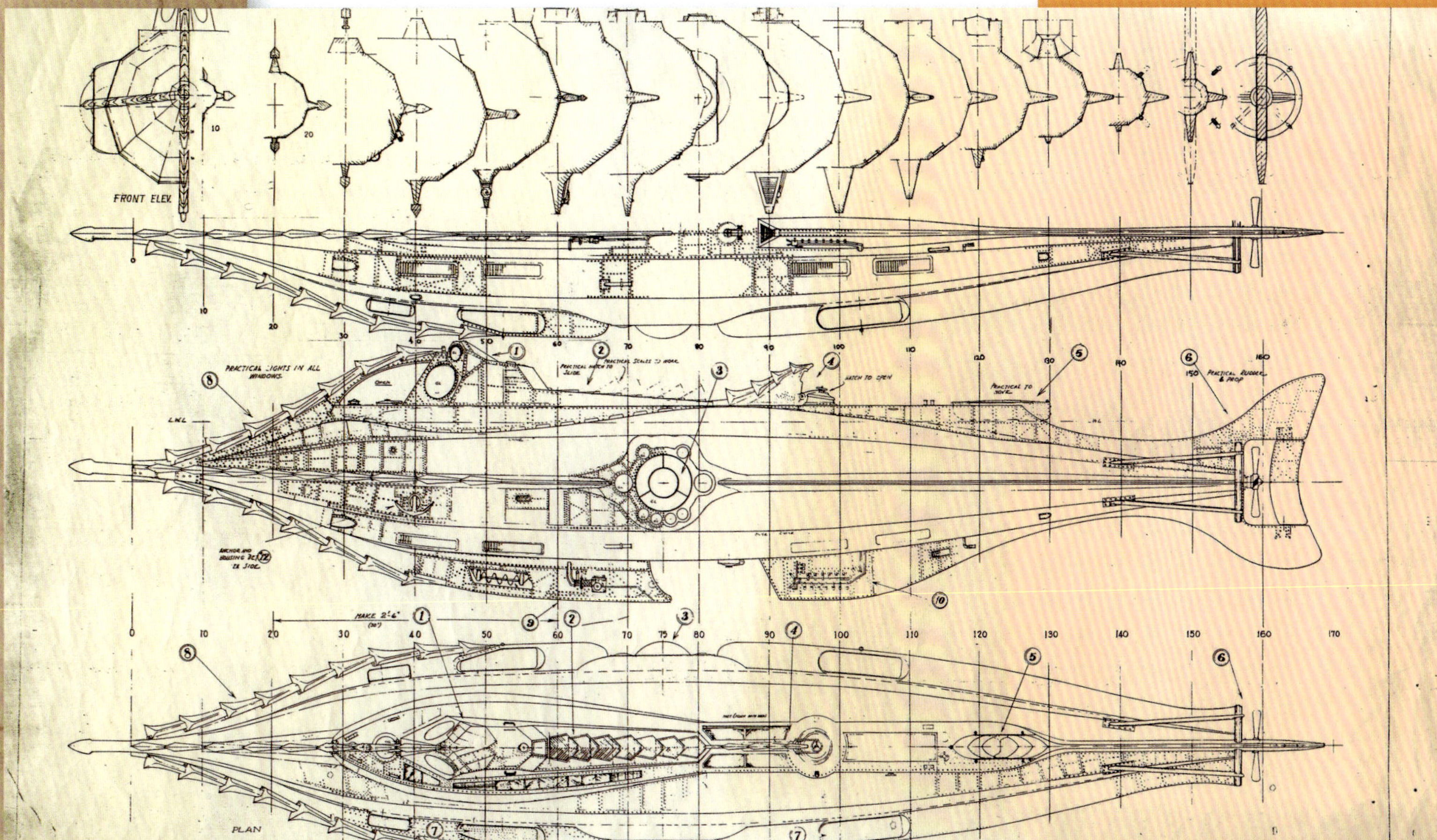

TOP Disney Studio Artist, design plans of the *Nautilus* for *20,000 Leagues Under the Sea* (1954); photocopy on paper

BOTTOM Harper Goff, *Nautilus* Concept Model II for *20,000 Leagues Under the Sea* (1954); plastic

OPPOSITE Disney Studio Artist, Concept Brownline plan of the *Nautilus* for *20,000 Leagues Under the Sea* (1954); printed ink on paper

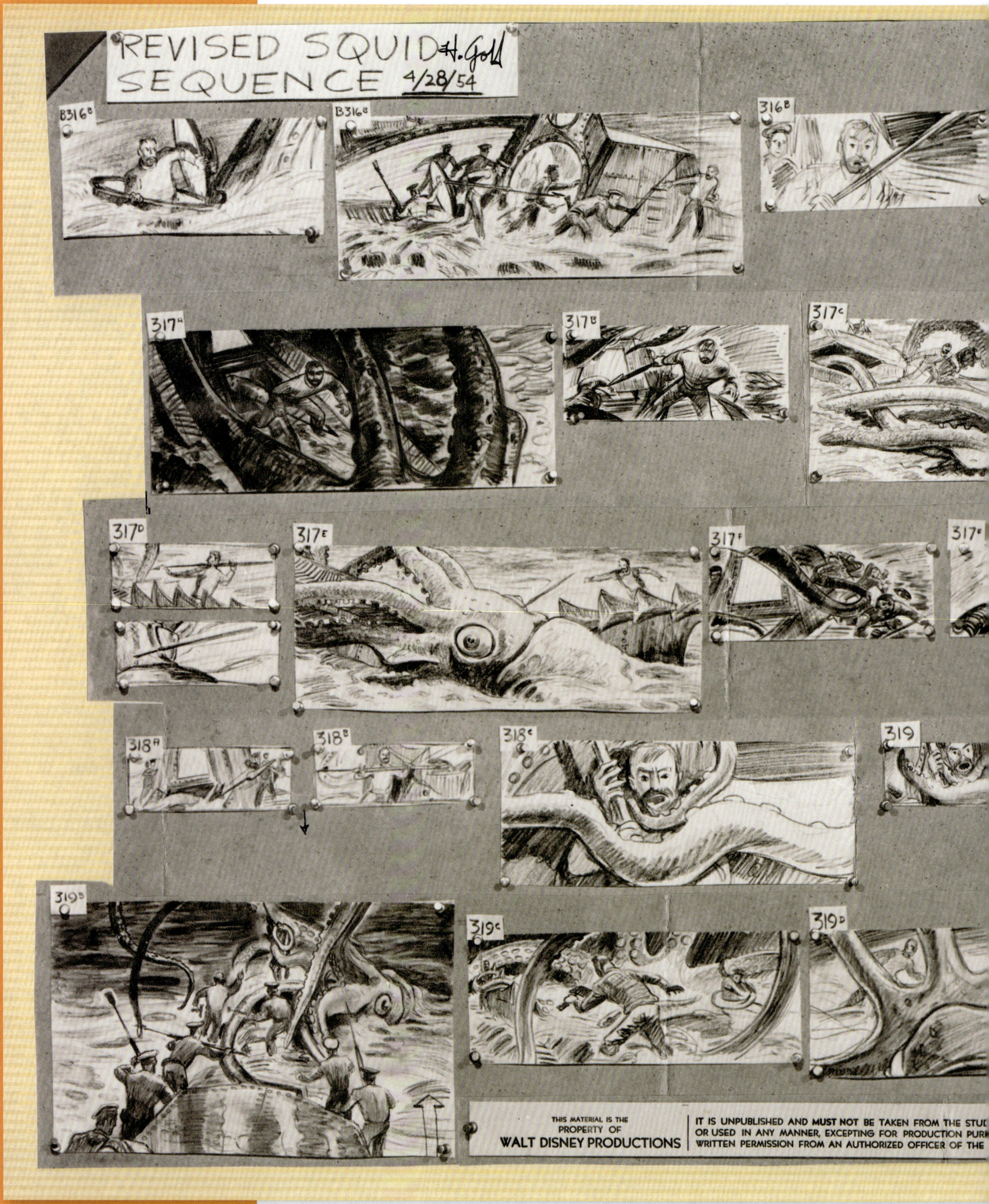
REVISED SQUID SEQUENCE H. Gold 4/28/54
B316B
B316C
316B
317A
317B
317C
317D
317E
317F
317
318A
318B
318C
319
319B
319C
319D
THIS MATERIAL IS THE PROPERTY OF WALT DISNEY PRODUCTIONS
IT IS UNPUBLISHED AND MUST NOT BE TAKEN FROM THE STUD
OR USED IN ANY MANNER, EXCEPTING FOR PRODUCTION PURP
WRITTEN PERMISSION FROM AN AUTHORIZED OFFICER OF THE

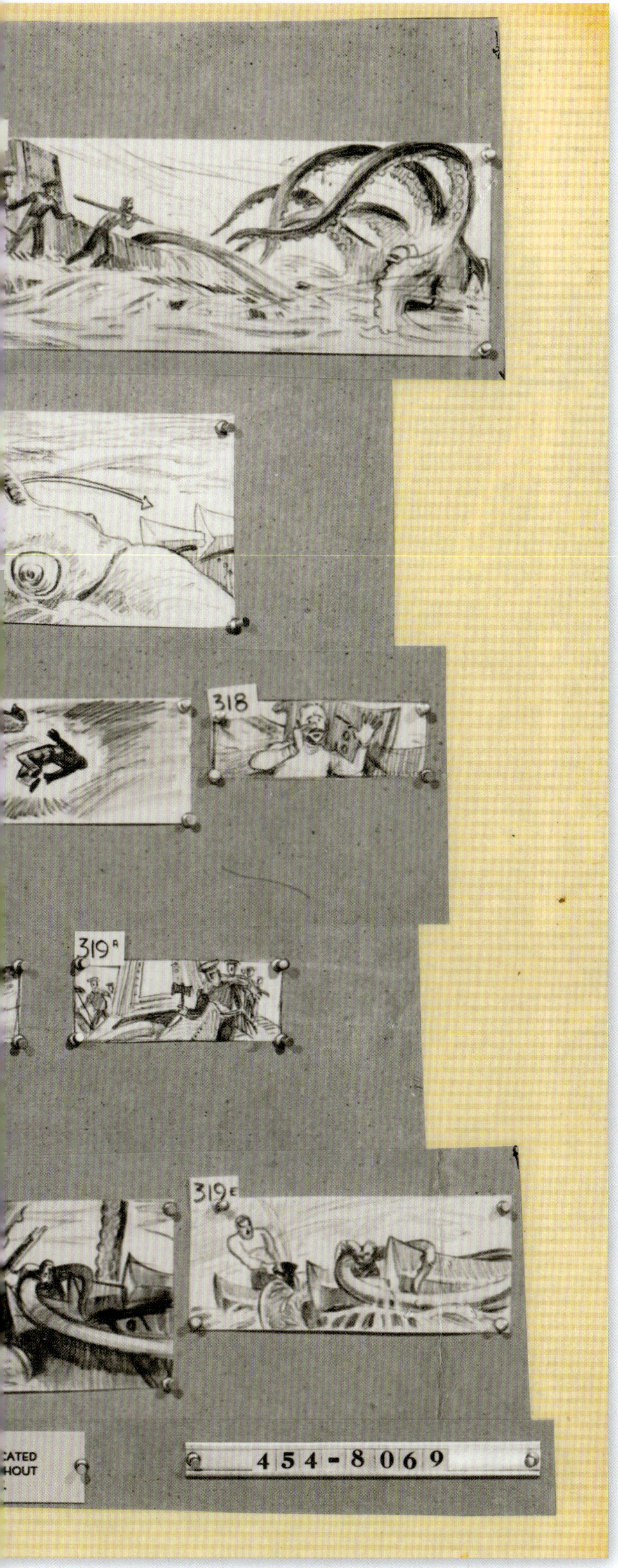

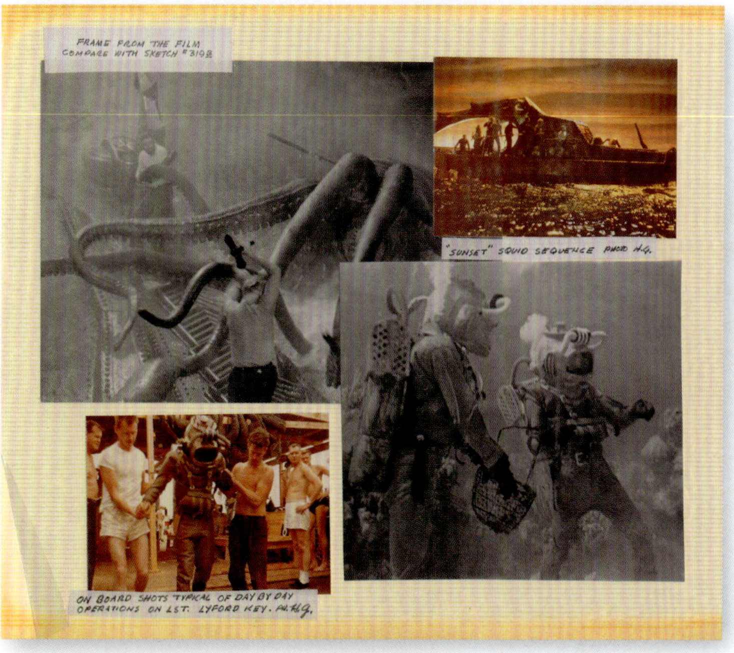

Harper Goff, scrapbook for *20,000 Leagues Under the Sea* (1954); photographs on paper

ARRIFLEX
16MM FILM CAMERA

EVEN AS EARLY AS THE 1940S AND 1950S, Walt was concerned about the environment. In searching to tell stories derived from the natural world for the silver screen, he enlisted a husband and wife team, Alfred and Elma Milotte, to go to Alaska. He requested they shoot everything they could. Walt studied the reels and zeroed in on footage of seals as being promising for a nature-focused film project. The resulting theatrical documentary, *Seal Island* (1948), won the Academy Award® for Best Short Subject.

Seal Island was the first in a series of thirteen films called True-Life Adventures, which documented the wonders of the natural world. The Millottes used the Arriflex camera to its full advantage, as Walt wrote for *The Atlantic* in 1954: "In Africa, operating from their specially built armored truck, the Millottes use the Arriflex camera with a 16-inch scope to bring the more savage quarry within safe range. The lioness who stalks and kills the wildebeest for a hungry family, seemingly only a few feet beyond the camera, was actually photographed some 800 yards away. Approached down-wind across the grassy plain by ... the great cat with her cubs and stalking aides never suspected a human observer." He continued, "The telephoto lens also brings to startling close-up the great African elephants in their family life around wilderness water holes and in the thorn bush pastures. The same lenses also serve for rhinos, hippos, giraffes, baboons, zebra, and other African quarry."

KODAK CINE SPECIAL
FILM CAMERA WITH 25MM LENS

ANOTHER IMPORTANT CAMERA USED to create the True-Life Adventures series was the Kodak Cine Special Camera. Cameraman Don Iwerks, son of Ub Iwerks, explained, "The True-Life Adventure films [were] photographed on Kodak 16mm Kodachrome film for three important reasons. First, the 16mm camera equipment is lightweight and portable. Second, the inexpensive 16mm film stock is ideal for unpredictable shooting conditions in the wild, where much film is wasted, and third, Kodachrome film records images that are very sharp and colorful that produce excellent 'blowups' to 35mm for exhibition in the theaters."

But while the photographers and state-of-the-art equipment were essential to create these films, "Nature remains the director," insisted Walt. "You can often set up your spying camera within a few yards of expected action. But only instinctive promptings, elemental urges, goad wild things to do what comes naturally." He continued, "The cameraman must be ready for the moment of revelation; often he has to depend on luck as well as advance preparation. Many of nature's finest and most exciting moments of action come with almost no warning. Wilderness creatures don't pose for their portraits. They cannot be directed. Human presence, especially among the larger ones, is just one more menace in their fear-haunted lives. So, the telescopic lens is a necessity in filming the more cautious, shy, or dangerous animals."

LEFT Arriflex 16 camera with 400mm Kilfitt lens adapter and baseplate, c. 1952; metal and wood

RIGHT Kodak Cine Special camera with 25mm lens and 100' magazine, c. 1948; metal and wood

MICKEY MOUSE CLUB
SET PROPS

ALWAYS LOOKING TO THE FUTURE of entertainment technology, Walt was an early adopter of broadcast television. After a few early television specials in the 1950s, Walt started the *Mickey Mouse Club* in 1955, and designed the show expressly for children. Unlike the movie theater-based clubs that had proliferated across the country in the 1930s, this "club" was a recurring weekday children's program. The series drew on the library of Disney cartoons but was dominated by original live-action material featuring a cast of children called the Mouseketeers. It also included new animated sequences, particularly featuring Jiminy Cricket. The cast, vetted through extensive auditions, were selected not only for talent but also for their naturalness and lack of show biz polish. They acquired a loyal following. The *Mickey Mouse Club* ran for four seasons before coming to an end. The original episodes continued to appear in syndication long after 1959.

Said Walt of the *Club*, "I feel I can do things with that *Mouse Club* that will be good entertainment, and constructive. I don't present a lot of nonsense to the children. I try to present sense in an entertaining way. My newsreel keeps children abreast of things going on around the world that interest children ... I don't believe in talking down to children."

MICKEY MOUSE CLUB

MOUSEKAVIKING HELMET

WHEN THIS HELMET, part of a one-of-a-kind set that included a related Viking spearhead, came into the Walt Disney Family Foundation Collection, its origins were originally a mystery. The two were separated and currently reside in different collections, The Walt Disney Family Museum and the Walt Disney Archives.

The Mousekavikings consisted of Ole Friis-Jensen, and Jorgen S. Jorgensen, both from Copenhagen, and Sten Blomqvist of Stockholm. In 1957, the three were attending the company's fourth annual International Merchandising Convention, hosted by Walt, Roy, and Walt Disney Productions (WDP) Character Merchandising Division. The attendees were WDP Character Merchandise representatives from around the world.

The spearhead was presented to the WDP team and the plaque that was adorned to the object reads, "1000 years old Viking spearhead dedicated to the great history teller of our time Walt Disney as a memorial of Scandinavia's great history makers of the past by the Mousekavikings at the Burbank convention 1957." A newspaper clipping documenting the convention featured Mousekavikings Ole Friis-Jensen, Jorgen S. Jorgensen, and Sten Blomqvist disembarking from a plane donning what appears to be the Mousekaviking helmets.

LEFT Mousekaviking helmet, 1957; metal and printed ink on paper

OPPOSITE LEFT Mickey Mouse Club member pin, c. 1955; plastic on metal

OPPOSITE RIGHT Candelario Delgado, Jimmie Dodd's Mousegetar, c. 1955; wood, string, and metal

WED ENTERPRISES

DISNEYLAND PROSPECTUS

THE RISE OF TELEVISION played a big part in Walt's idea for Disneyland. Said Walt, "Every time I'd get thinking of television I would think of this park. And I knew that if I did anything like the park that I had to have some kind of a medium like television to let the people know about it ... I had a contract that said I had complete say of what we produced. So, I just sort of insisted that my Disneyland Park be a part of my television."

In fall 1953, while preparing for a meeting with potential investors, Walt recruited Herb Ryman, a former Disney studio artist, to create a special bird's-eye concept drawing of his proposed park. Ryman worked closely with Walt to translate his ideas onto paper.

The Disneyland Prospectus was a pitch document designed to help Walt raise money to build Disneyland. The pitch opens by saying, "Like Alice stepping Through the Looking Glass, to step through the portals of DISNEYLAND will be like entering another world." Inside it details the layout of the Park, what attractions you could find in each land, the types of merchandise and food options that would be offered, as well as seasonal offerings. The layout of Disneyland in the early stages included lands that would evolve into something different like "Lilliputian Land" also described as "A Land of Little Things," and "Recreation Land," described as "A Leisure Land." These would eventually evolve into other, more familiar, lands.

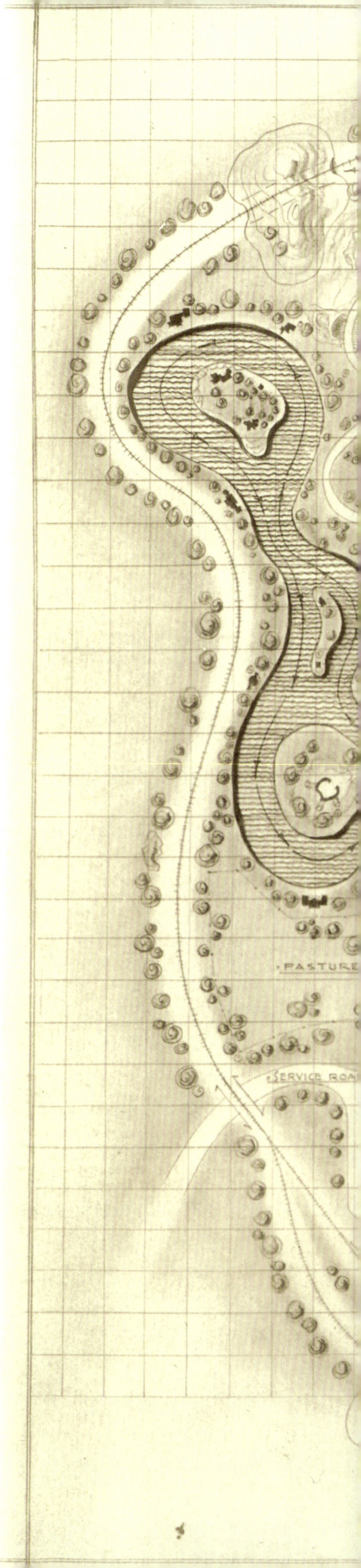

OPPOSITE Disneyland Prospectus, proposed layout drawing, 1953; printed ink on paper, and colored pencil and watercolor on paper

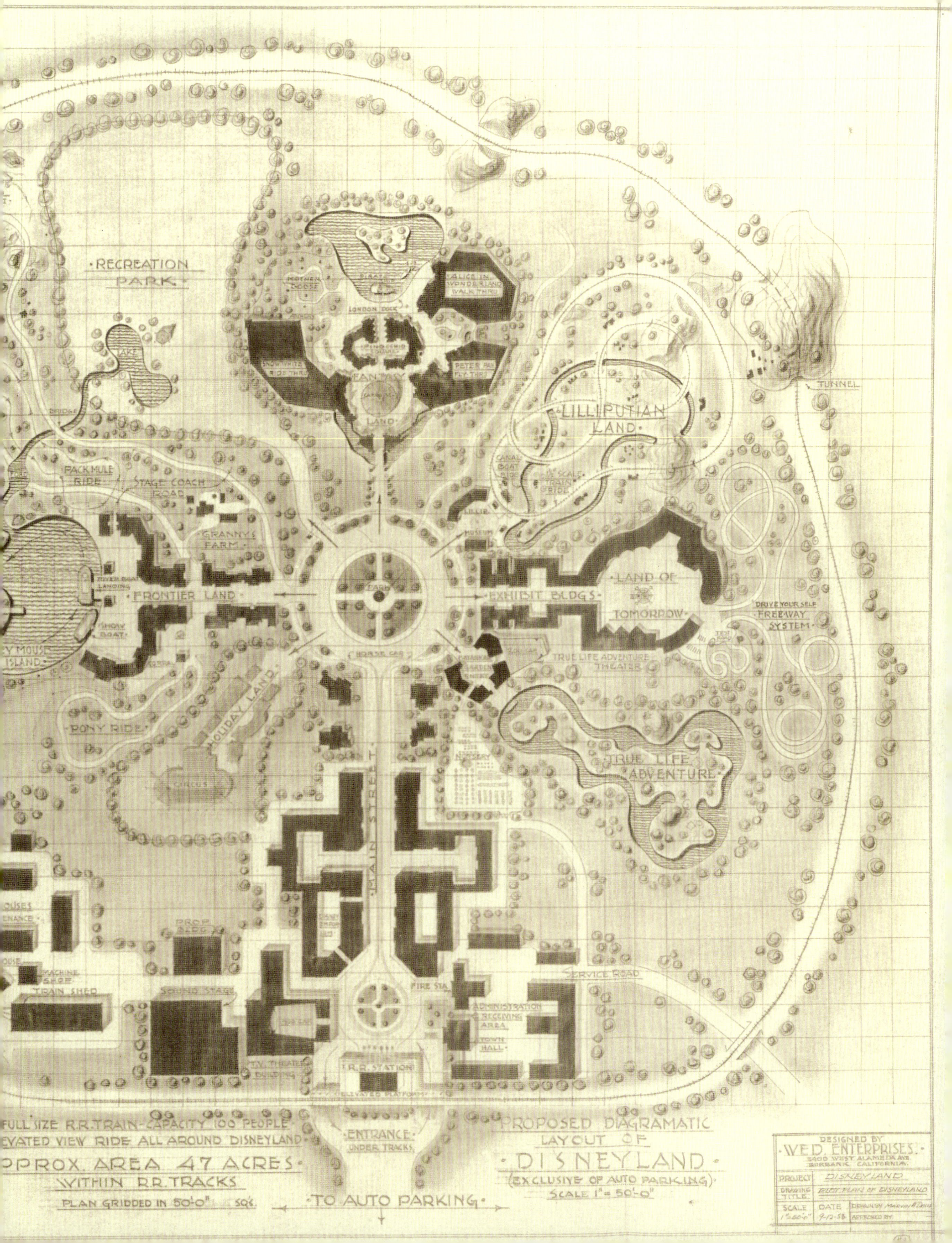

RECREATION PARK
LAKE
PACKMULE RIDE
STAGE COACH ROAD
GRANNY'S FARM
RIVER BOAT LANDING
SHOW BOAT
FRONTIER LAND
PONY RIDE
HOLIDAY LAND
CIRCUS
MOTHER GOOSE
PIRATE SHIP
LONDON DOCK
ALICE IN WONDERLAND WALK THRU
SNOW WHITE RIDE THRU
PETER PAN FLY THRU
FANTASY LAND
LILLIPUTIAN LAND
CANAL BOAT RIDE
SCALE TRAIN RIDE
MUSEUM
PARK
EXHIBIT BLDGS
LAND OF TOMORROW
TUNNEL
DRIVE YOUR SELF FREE-WAY SYSTEM
HORSE CAR
TRUE LIFE ADVENTURE THEATER
TRUE LIFE ADVENTURE
MAIN STREET
PROP BLDG.
MACHINE SHOP
TRAIN SHED
SOUND STAGE
T.V. THEATER BUILDING
FIRE STA.
ADMINISTRATION & RECEIVING AREA
TOWN HALL
R.R. STATION
SERVICE ROAD
FULL SIZE R.R. TRAIN-CAPACITY 100 PEOPLE
EVATED VIEW RIDE ALL AROUND DISNEYLAND
ENTRANCE UNDER TRACKS
PPROX. AREA 47 ACRES
WITHIN R.R. TRACKS
PLAN GRIDDED IN 50'-0" SQ'S.
TO AUTO PARKING
PROPOSED DIAGRAMATIC LAYOUT OF
DISNEYLAND
(EXCLUSIVE OF AUTO PARKING)
SCALE 1" = 50'-0"
DESIGNED BY
W.E.D. ENTERPRISES.
3400 WEST ALAMEDA AVE
BURBANK CALIFORNIA.
PROJECT DISNEYLAND
DRAWING TITLE PLOT PLAN OF DISNEYLAND
SCALE 1" = 50'-0"
DATE 9-12-53
DRAWN BY MARVIN A DAVIS
APPROVED BY

PART 3

INSPIRATION

Walt Disney began his life's work as an artist, and the artistic influences that he encountered in his youth continued to impact his work throughout his career. Walt cultivated a wide-ranging interest in art throughout his life—one that extended far beyond the consistent, family-friendly aesthetic of the Studios' productions. As a filmmaker, Walt humbly recognized his artistic shortcomings while simultaneously pushing forward his chosen field as an art form. "To tell you the truth," he said, "I was never a good artist. I was never satisfied with what I did, but it was a means to an end."

Recognizing the limits of his own artistic abilities, Walt had the exceptional talent of seeing the potential in others. He recruited artists to his studio and directed the talents of his employees. In turn, the Studios' output began exerting influence externally into what was considered "fine art," a trend that began in Walt's Hollywood career and continues today. More than eighty artists—most famously Andy Warhol, Peter Max, Takashi Murakami, and Roy Lichtenstein—have been inspired by and even used images of Disney characters or images in their own art.

This is one of my Original
Drawings WINSOR McCAY—
92

WINSOR MCCAY

THE SINKING OF THE LUSITANIA (1918) FILM CEL

WINSOR MCCAY WAS A PIONEERING American cartoonist and animator who worked under the pen name Silas on the comic strip "Dream of the Rarebit Fiend." He was a prolific artist and his pioneering early animated films far outshone the work of his contemporaries. His films set a standard followed by Walt and others in later decades. He produced beautifully elaborate films, such as *Little Nemo* (1911) and *The Sinking of the Lusitania* (1918).

The Sinking of the Lusitania was a World War I propaganda film that recreated the 1915 sinking of the British liner RMS *Lusitania*. The short film highlighted animation's unique potential, giving vision and movement to an event where no photographers were present. At twelve minutes, this was the longest work of animation at the time of its release. Today, the film is the earliest surviving animated documentary and dramatic work of animation. Animated films were originally created using cellulose nitrate film cels, which are prone to spontaneous combustion and would often melt under excessive heat. With innovations in filmmaking, animation cels were improved so they wouldn't deteriorate as quickly. This cel from the film has survived over a century, and it is remarkably rare to see the celluloid in this condition. This cel setup is inscribed by McCay, "This is one of my original drawings / Winsor McCay."

"Winsor McCay and other animation novelties stimulated a great public interest and created a demand for this new medium. This in turn encouraged other pioneers to creative efforts that in time led to the establishment of the animated cartoon as an industry."

—WALT

OPPOSITE Winsor McCay, cel from *The Sinking of the Lusitania* (1918); ink on celluloid

E. G. LUTZ

ANIMATED CARTOONS

BELOW Edwin George "E. G." Lutz, *Animated Cartoons*, 1920; printed ink on paper

OPPOSITE TOP Walt Pfeiffer, *Happy Landing, Walt!*; ink and possibly watercolor or gouache on paper

OPPOSITE BOTTOM Walt and Walt Pfeiffer in Chaplin-inspired dress, c. 1913

WHEN WALT WAS FIRST INTRODUCED to animation while working at Kansas City Film Ad, he started doing his own research into the art of animation. He searched for materials created by film pioneers, such as Eadweard Muybridge and E. G. Lutz. Walt Disney was a lifelong reader and credited E. G. Lutz's book, *Animated Cartoons*, with teaching him the fundamentals of animation. Said Walt of the book, "It wasn't very profound. It was just something the guy had put together to make a buck but still there are ideas in there. I have always felt there was a need of a good story on animation for other guys like myself."

The book served as a helpful starting point for Walt during his early experimentations with animation. Later in his career, it would become inspiration for his own book, *The Art of Animation*, written by journalist Bob Thomas and the staff of the Walt Disney Studio. The book details many of the Disney feature films and shorts up to 1958, during the production of *Sleeping Beauty* (1959). It is broken up into sections highlighting story, characters, sound, music, direction, layout, animation, background, color, and the future of animation. *The Art of Animation* would go on to inspire countless following generations of artists and animators.

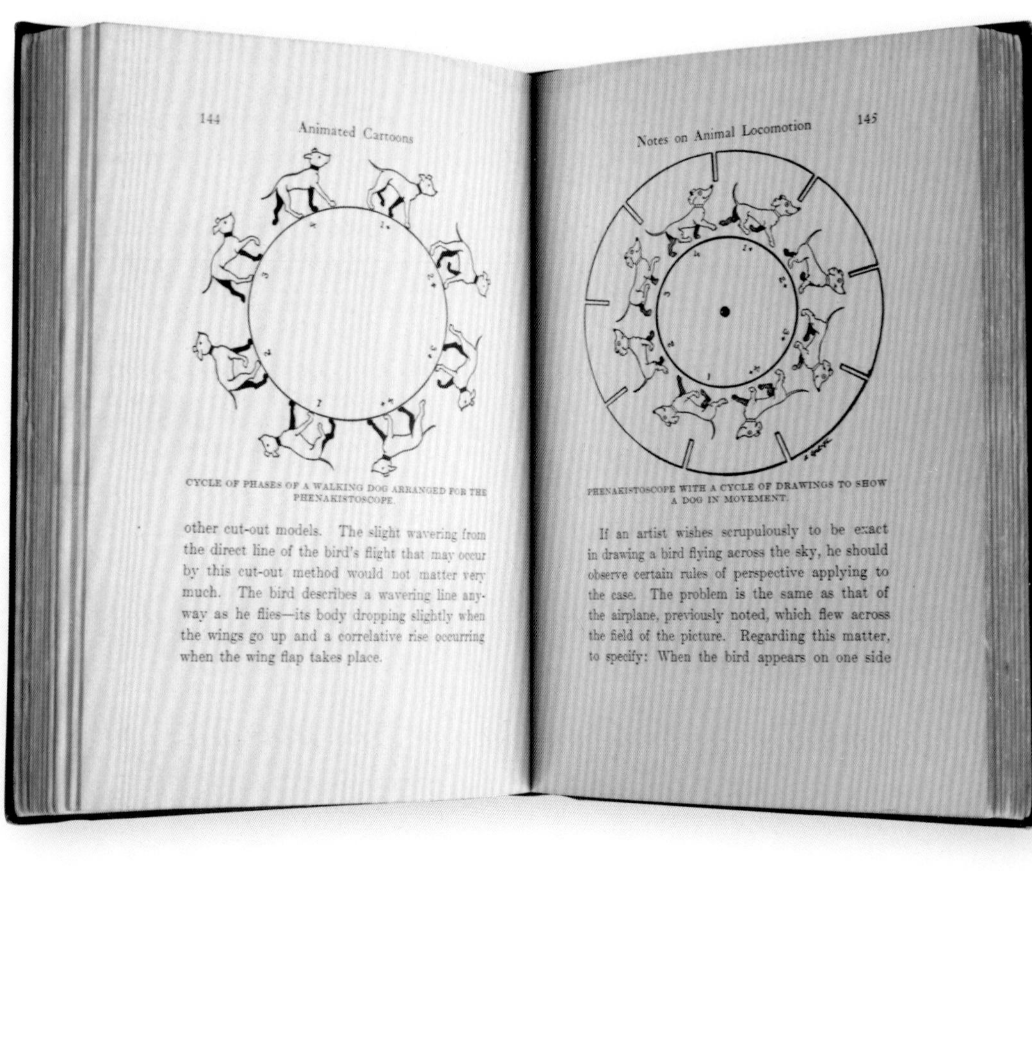

144 Animated Cartoons

CYCLE OF PHASES OF A WALKING DOG ARRANGED FOR THE PHENAKISTOSCOPE.

other cut-out models. The slight wavering from the direct line of the bird's flight that may occur by this cut-out method would not matter very much. The bird describes a wavering line anyway as he flies—its body dropping slightly when the wings go up and a correlative rise occurring when the wing flap takes place.

Notes on Animal Locomotion 145

PHENAKISTOSCOPE WITH A CYCLE OF DRAWINGS TO SHOW A DOG IN MOVEMENT.

If an artist wishes scrupulously to be exact in drawing a bird flying across the sky, he should observe certain rules of perspective applying to the case. The problem is the same as that of the airplane, previously noted, which flew across the field of the picture. Regarding this matter, to specify: When the bird appears on one side

WALT PFEIFFER'S

CARICATURE OF WALT DISNEY

WALTER PFEIFFER WAS ONE OF MANY of Walt Disney's colleagues who made the move to Hollywood from Kansas City and "The Two Walts" were lifelong friends. He was employed by Walt Disney Productions in various capacities from 1935 until his retirement in 1972. Walt met the young Walter Pfeiffer while attending primary school in Kansas City. He cemented his friendship with his schoolmate when he went to visit the Pfieffer household and heard Walter had the mumps. Since Walt had already had them and was therefore immune, he was allowed to visit. Walt brought paper and charcoal to show Walter how to draw.

This stylized depiction of Walt Disney on horseback playing polo was created by Pfeiffer. The rider, wearing a yellow "Mickey" polo shirt, concentrates on finding the ball, while his sleek black horse appears to rear up slightly. Polo played an important part in Walt's life, providing stress relief and exercise as he captained the studio's players, known as the Mickey Mouse team.

The Pfeiffer family home became very influential to a young Walt Disney, and he considered it one of his early "laughing place[s]." He was introduced to vaudeville shows and motion pictures. Intrigued by the newfound form of entertainment, Walt and Walter would act out the jokes and songs they heard in the shows in their own local performances.

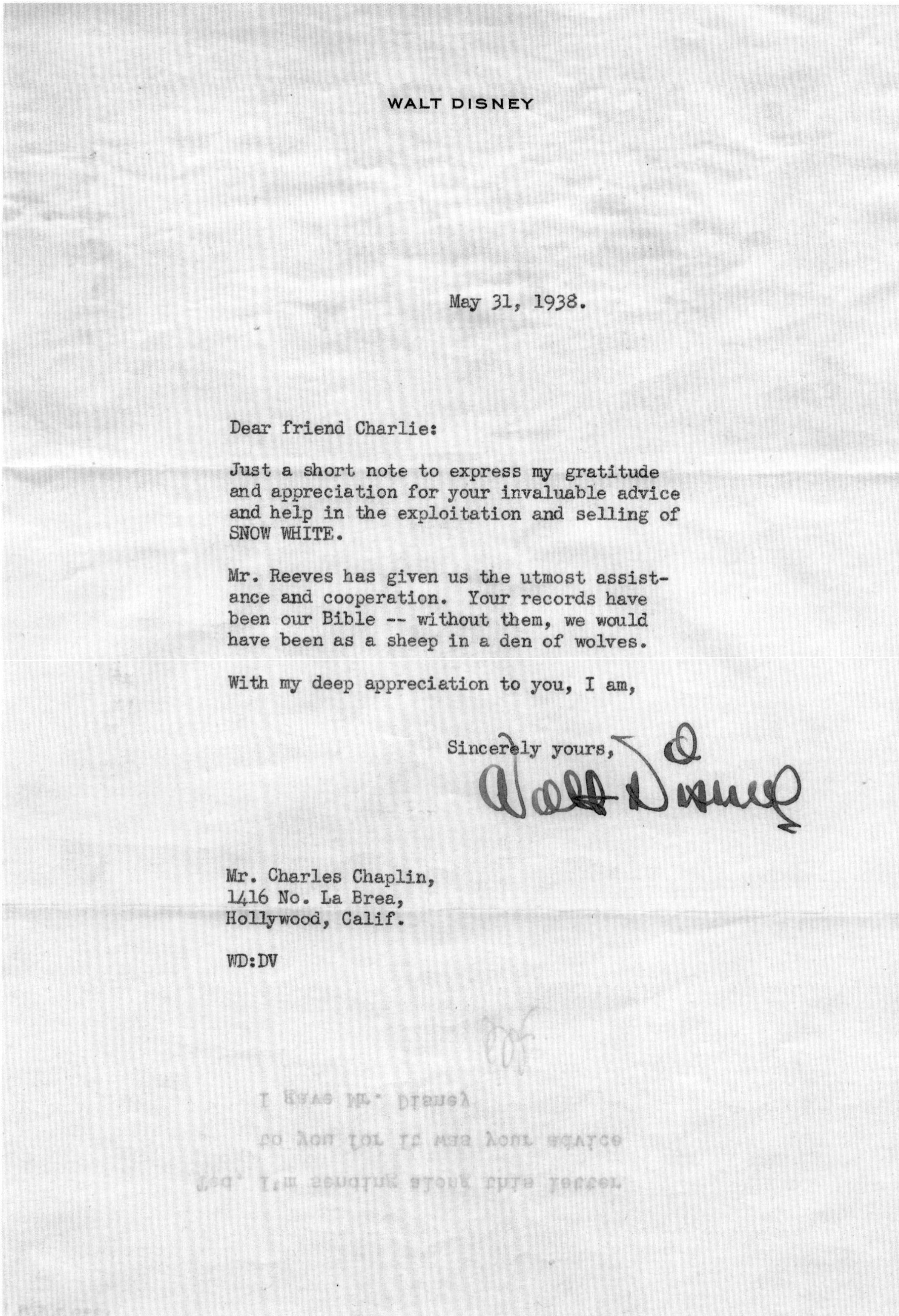

WALT DISNEY

May 31, 1938.

Dear friend Charlie:

Just a short note to express my gratitude and appreciation for your invaluable advice and help in the exploitation and selling of SNOW WHITE.

Mr. Reeves has given us the utmost assistance and cooperation. Your records have been our Bible -- without them, we would have been as a sheep in a den of wolves.

With my deep appreciation to you, I am,

Sincerely yours,

Mr. Charles Chaplin,
1416 No. La Brea,
Hollywood, Calif.

WD:DV

WALT'S

LETTER TO CHARLIE CHAPLIN

CHARLIE CHAPLIN WAS A CHILDHOOD INSPIRATION who would go on to become a lifelong friend of Walt and would help inspire the character of Mickey Mouse. In 1931, Walt recalled, "I think we were rather indebted to Charlie Chaplin for the idea. We wanted something appealing, and we thought of a tiny bit of a mouse that would have something of the wistfulness of Chaplin, a little fellow trying to do the best he could."

Chaplin attended the 1937 premiere of *Snow White and the Seven Dwarfs* (1937). He later told the *Los Angeles Times* that the character of Dopey was "one of the greatest comedians of all time." In this letter from Disney to Chaplin, Walt wrote on May 31, 1938, "Just a short note to express my gratitude and appreciation for your invaluable advice and help in the exploitation and selling of SNOW WHITE."

Walt and Chaplin developed a personal relationship over the years. "Charlie Chaplin was a friend," Walt recalled in 1956. Chaplin gave Walt the helpful counsel, "Your pictures are going to live a long time. My advice to you is to clear and buy up every one of your pictures. If there's any that you don't own, get out and buy 'em."

OPPOSITE Letter to Charlie Chaplin from Walt, 1938; handwritten and printed ink on paper

BELOW Walt and Charlie Chaplin, late 1930s

GENERAL JOHN J. PERSHING

MEMOIR SET

GENERAL OF THE ARMIES OF THE UNITED STATES, John "Black Jack" Pershing was the commander of the 8th Brigade in the Presidio of San Francisco in 1914, before being dispatched to the Mexican border to pursue military leader Pancho Villa.

During Walt's time volunteering as a chauffeur for the American Red Cross, General Pershing sent his ten-year-old son Warren to visit his good friend Alice Howell, who managed the canteen in Nancy, France, and Walt was assigned to drive the boy.

In 1931, when Walt and Lillian visited Washington, D.C., the publicist at their hotel recognized Walt and asked if there were any arrangements that could be made for the couple during their stay. Walt shared that he would like to meet General Pershing. An appointment with General Pershing proved impossible, but in lieu of his presence Pershing sent this set of autographed copies of his memoirs, *My Experiences in the World War,* Volumes 1–2. The first volume is inscribed "For Walt Disney A.E.F. [American Expeditionary Forces] / wondering if he thought out Mickey Mouse while serving in France and with best wishes 1935 / John J. Pershing." In 1932, Pershing was awarded the Pulitzer Prize for history for the two-volume memoirs.

BELOW AND OPPOSITE
John J. Pershing, *My Experiences in the World War*, Volume I, 1931; leather and handwritten and printed ink on paper

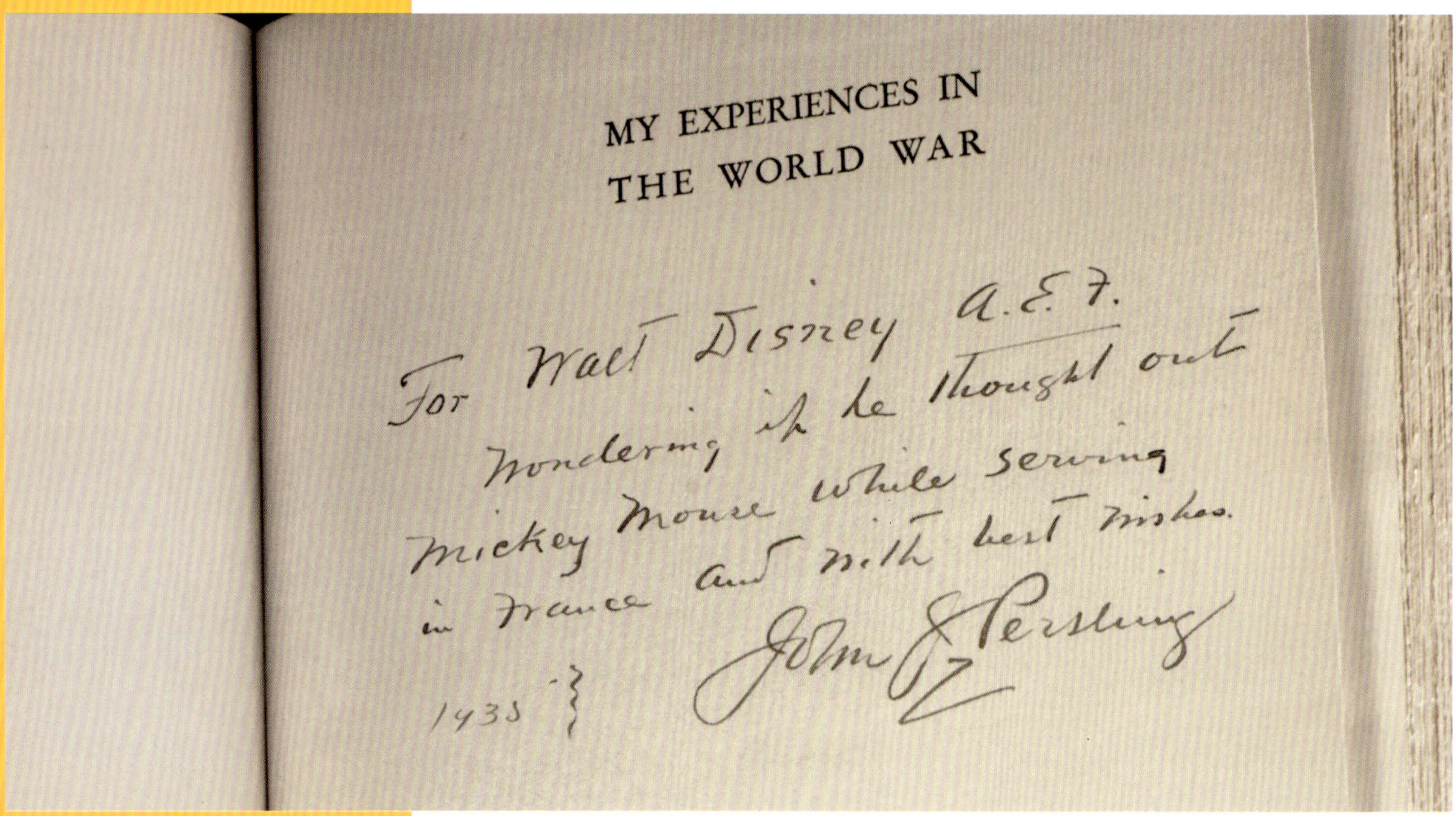

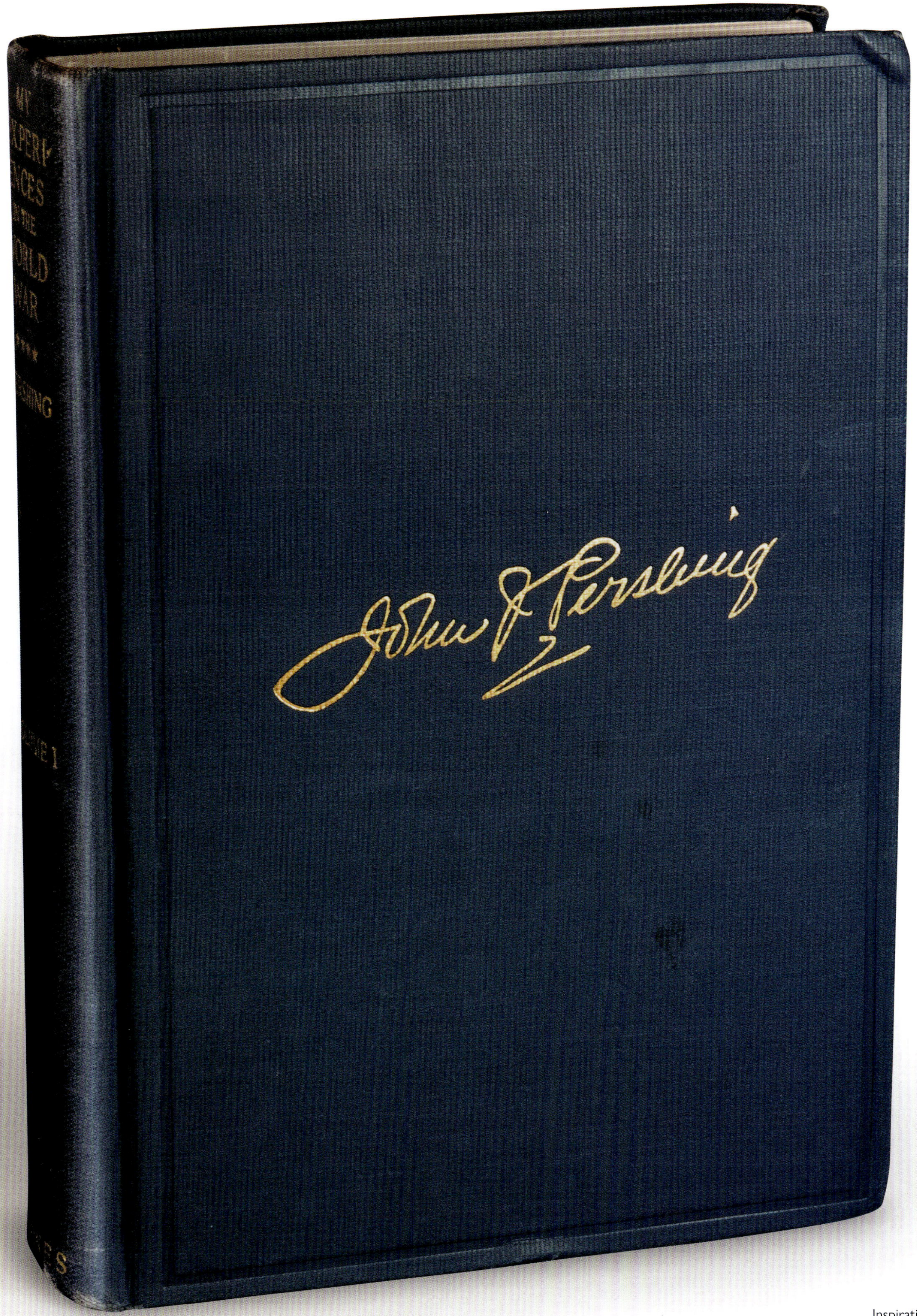

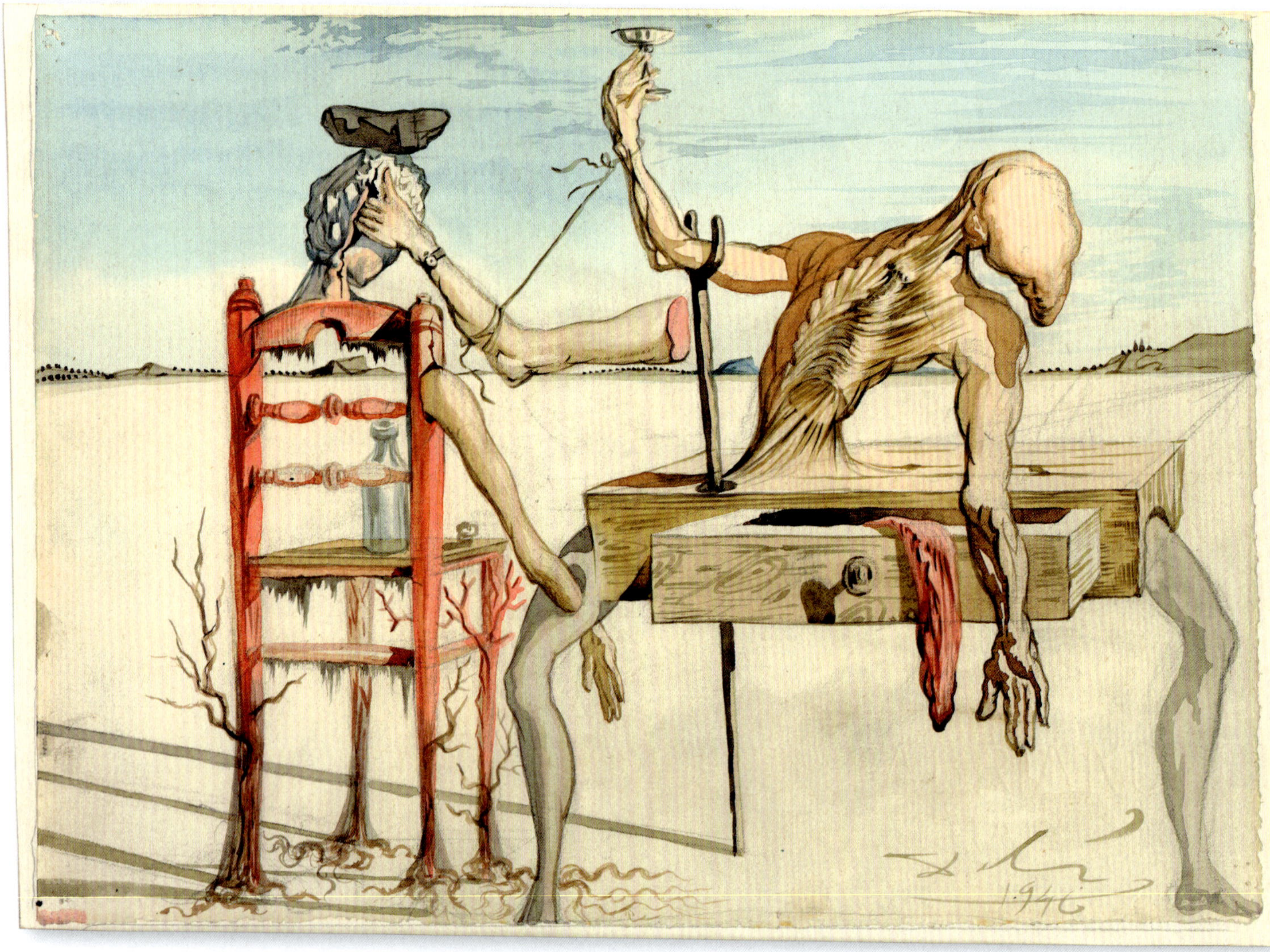

WALT'S

SALVADOR DALÍ WATERCOLOR

AFTER READING DALÍ'S AUTOBIOGRAPHY, *The Secret Life of Salvador Dalí*, Disney sent his copy to the artist asking for not only his autograph but also a suggestion of a collaboration with The Walt Disney Studios. World War II would put an association between the two men on hold, but in 1945 Disney engaged Dalí to design a surrealistic animated short to be a segment of a packaged film. The short was called *Destino*, the Spanish word for "destiny." Starting in January 1946, Dalí spent his time between Pebble Beach, California, and The Walt Disney Studios in Burbank, California, writing outlines and treatments, clarifying his ideas, balancing the weights between animation and live-action, drawing, and relentlessly working side by side with Disney personnel on this extraordinary collaboration. Over time, however, it became more apparent that there were differences in the two men's approach to storytelling and by 1948, work would cease on *Destino*.

Despite the disappointing end of the *Destino* project, the friendship between Disney and Dalí endured through the coming decades. Walt adorned the walls of his Palm Springs home with Dalí's paintings. The pair would also visit each other in their homes throughout the years.

WALT'S PERSONAL COPY OF

SALVADOR DALÍ'S INSCRIBED COPY OF *MACBETH*

SINCE THE LATE 1930S, Walt had expressed interest in producing an animated version of *Don Quixote*. Both eternal optimists, he and Dalí shared the dream of working together to bring the classic epic tale to life. In Walt's personal library, this 1946 edition of William Shakespeare's *Macbeth* was found with an illustration by Dalí, which Dalí playfully signed with a drawing of Don Quixote. Accompanying the illustration Dalí wrote, "Pour Mon Tres Cher Ami, Walt Disney Bonjour! Dalí," which translates from French, "For my very dear friend, Walt Disney, good day!"

On a trip to California in 1951, Dalí visited Disney's home and rode his 1/8-scale steam train, the Carolwood Pacific Railroad. That same year, interoffice memos and a Disney-issued press release announced that *Don Quixote* was going into production as a live-action film.

In 1957, Disney and his wife, Lillian, visited the Dalís in Portlligat, Spain, where they discussed *Don Quixote* and another of Dalí's pet projects, the epic story of the medieval Spanish hero El Cid. Unfortunately, neither project was ever realized.

THIS PAGE Walt's personal copy of William Shakespeare's *Macbeth* with an illustration and inscription of *Don Quixote de la Mancha* by Salvador Dalí, 1946; handwritten and printed ink on paper

OPPOSITE TOP Salvador Dalí, *Untitled*, 1946; watercolor on paper

OPPOSITE BOTTOM Walt and Salvador Dalí in Spain, 1957

BELOW Diego Rivera, "Mickey Mouse and American Art" essay, 1931; handwritten ink on paper

OPPOSITE Pamela Lyndon "P. L." Travers, *Mary Poppins* book, 1934; printed ink on paper

DIEGO RIVERA ESSAY

"MICKEY MOUSE AND AMERICAN ART"

IN FEBRUARY 1932, the internationally acclaimed Mexican painter and muralist, Diego Rivera, published a 600-word essay, "Mickey Mouse and American Art," in a New York literary and artistic journal, *Contact*. Here is the original nine-page handwritten essay on hotel letterhead.

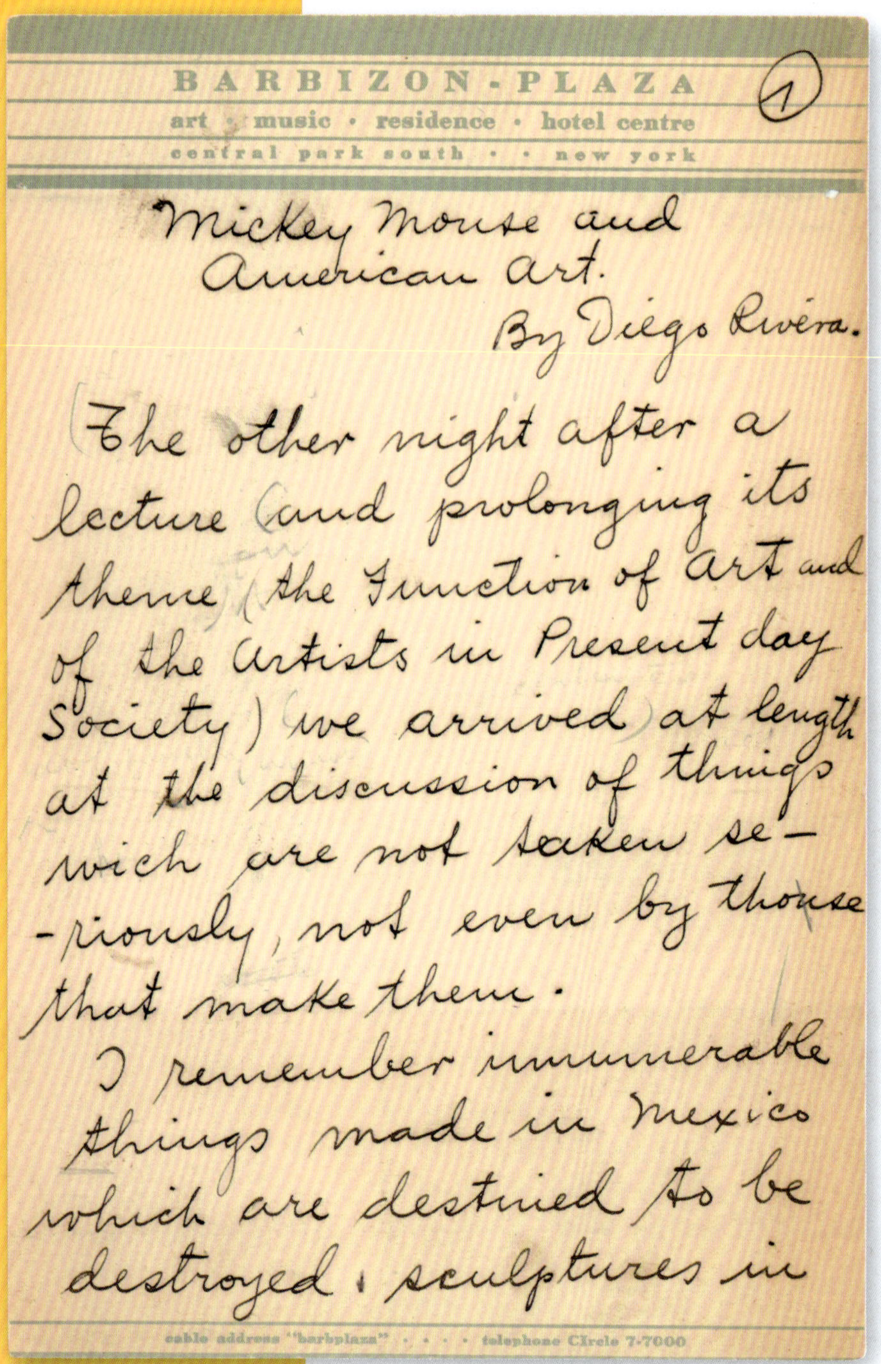
BARBIZON-PLAZA
art · music · residence · hotel centre
central park south · · new york
(1)

Mickey Mouse and
American art.
By Diego Rivera.

The other night after a lecture (and prolonging its theme (the Function of art and of the artists in Present day Society) we arrived at length at the discussion of things wich are not taken se-riously, not even by thouse that make them.

I remember innumerable things made in Mexico which are destined to be destroyed; sculptures in

cable address "barbplaza" · · · · telephone Circle 7-7000

In the essay, Rivera extols Mickey Mouse and his cartoon pals as "the genuine heroes of American art in the first half of the 20th century." He predicts that, after the revolution, cartoons—with their standardized drawing, clear messaging, and predetermined meanings—would be the people's most beloved medium.

Rivera's article ends abruptly, with no real discussion of the character. We may never know what else, if anything, he might have said about "Mickey Mouse and American Art," or, for that matter, Walt Disney. But we do know that they did meet. During Walt's trip for the United States goodwill tour through South America in 1942, they were pictured together at the opening of a nightclub in Mexico City, in the company of Mexican film star Dolores del Rio.

At the time, a prediction like Diego Rivera's that Mickey was destined to be one of "the genuine heroes of American art in the first half of the 20th century," might have been dismissed as preposterous. But in the fullness of time Mickey Mouse did, in fact, become the most iconic American artistic creation ever.

WALT'S COPY OF

MARY POPPINS BY P. L. TRAVERS

AFTER ITS FIRST PUBLICATION, Walt received a copy of P. L. Travers' *Mary Poppins* inscribed by its American publisher Eugene Reynal: "To Walt Disney—Not another 'Mickey' but I think you should like our Mary." And like her he did, as did his daughters. Walt's daughter Diane, in particular, enjoyed reading *Mary Poppins*, inspiring him to pursue film adaptation rights.

Although Walt found the story of the beloved English nanny to be perfect material for a Disney film, Travers didn't agree. As early as 1944, Walt tried to secure the film rights to the book, but it took more than fifteen years before he succeeded. Eventually Travers was won over, but not without Walt first granting her final script approval. Even with that concession, however, the author historically wavered on her satisfaction with the final product, though the public and critics felt otherwise.

Mary Poppins (1964) went on to become one of The Walt Disney Studios' greatest successes. The film earned thirteen Academy Award® nominations. While it didn't win for Best Picture, the film did walk away with five Oscars®, including Best Actress for its star, Julie Andrews, and for Best Musical Score, composed by Walt's famous songwriting duo, Richard and Robert Sherman.

COLLECTION OF
HEINRICH KLEY ARTWORKS

WALT DISNEY REGULARLY LOOKED to European art for inspiration and used those influences to inform story development central to a film's visual concepts. Using elements drawn from traditional European artworks and storybook illustrations, in particular, Walt encouraged his animators to be inspired and adapt those elements to create unique and influential visual narratives.

On a trip to Europe in 1935, Walt acquired 335 illustrated books and additional artworks to serve as inspiration for animators on future Disney projects. These included works by German artist Heinrich Kley, who became one of Walt's favorite illustrators. In a 1964 television interview, Walt said, "Without the wonderful drawings of Heinrich Kley, I could not conduct my art school classes for my animators."

Kley's influence resonates in classic Disney films such as *Peter Pan* (1953) and *Dumbo* (1941), but his work is most reflected in the demons of "Night on Bald Mountain" and the anthropomorphic animals in "The Dance of the Hours" from *Fantasia* (1940). The menacing Chernabog in "Night on Bald Mountain" is deeply influenced by Kley's work *Jugend Titelblatt* (Title Page of Youth), c. 1920, where the painting depicts two demons lording over a mechanical factory, turning it into their own industrial playground.

Heinrich Kley's influence on the Disney visual aesthetic is unmistakable. Like Kley, Disney artists now inspire future generations to continue the tradition of infusing creative processes with compelling art.

BELOW Heinrich Kley, *Boxende Hasen* (Boxing Rabbits), c. 1920; ink on paper

OPPOSITE Heinrich Kley, *Jugend Titelblatt* (Title Page of Youth), c. 1910; gouache on paper

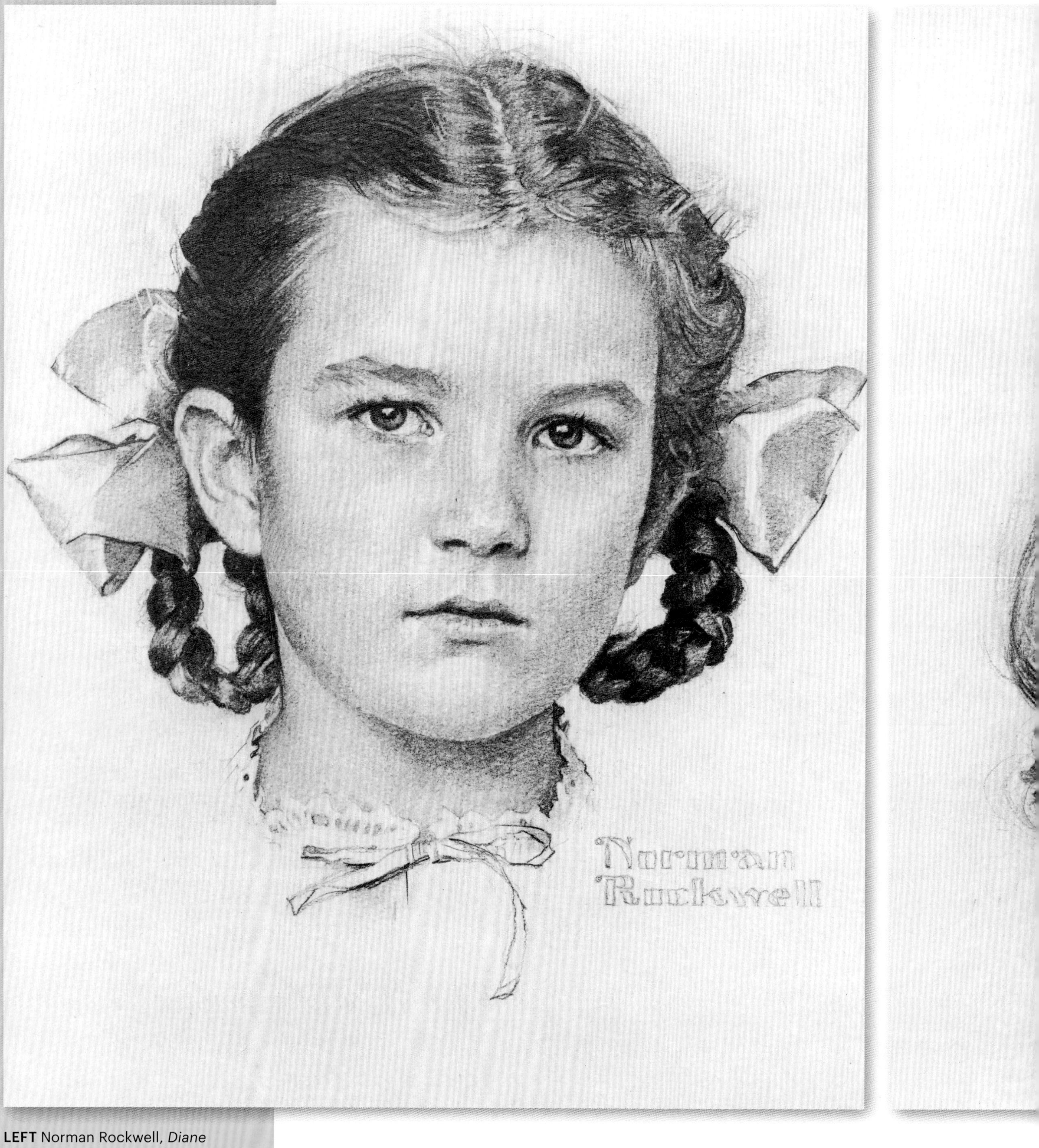

LEFT Norman Rockwell, *Diane Disney*, 1941; charcoal on paper

RIGHT Norman Rockwell, *Sharon Disney*, 1941; charcoal on paper

NORMAN ROCKWELL

PORTRAITS OF DIANE AND SHARON

WHILE TRAVELING IN NEW ENGLAND IN THE LATE 1930S, Walt, Lillian, her sister Hazel, and Hazel's husband Bill Cottrell stopped for lunch at a tearoom. Inside were framed pictures by Norman Rockwell. Walt asked the waitress if Rockwell lived in the area and the waitress gave directions to his home. Cottrell remembers, "The four of us [went] over and there's Norman Rockwell, cutting [the] lawn. ... Of course, Walt knew him. He was glad to see Walt. Went inside his barn, where his studio was up in the loft there."

Walt and Rockwell corresponded over the years. In 1941, Walt commissioned him to draw portraits of his two daughters, ten-year-old Diane and seven-year-old Sharon. In preparation for the charcoal portraits, Rockwell visited Walt's office at the Disney Studios and took reference photographs of his daughters. "I was ... a real brat about it," Diane laughed.

The portraits of Diane and Sharon hung prominently in Walt's office for more than two decades. After his passing, the individual portraits went to the family homes of each daughter, where the originals reside today.

Diane's daughter Tamara recalled, "My mother's Norman Rockwell portrait is a priceless portrayal of her as a very young girl. With her braids and bows, and an expression both serene and serious, I can only imagine what she was thinking. I was lucky enough to have her pass it on to me, as she said that I resembled her the most. I have always felt honored to be able to look at it every day, as well as feeling equally honored to resemble her."

NEYSA MCMEIN

PORTRAIT OF DIANE

THIS PORTRAIT OF A SIXTEEN-YEAR-OLD DIANE DISNEY MILLER holding a copy of *Alice in Wonderland* (the Disney adaptation of Lewis Carroll's *Alice in Wonderland* would be released two years later) was painted by significant illustrator and portrait painter Neysa McMein. A smaller copy of the painting sat on top of the piano in Walt's studio office.

While working, McMein sent an update to Walt about the status of the portrait. She noted, "Having a chance to study it in a good light I have put the background in ... but didn't want to send it off until I got a criticism from a couple of artists here. Also, I want the curator of Fine Arts from the Met to pass on it which will do the first of the week." The portrait was unfortunately left unfinished due to the unexpected passing of McMein in 1949.

Neysa McMein was known for creating important posters for the U.S. government and the American Red Cross during World War I. She also created illustrations for magazines and painted the first iconic version of Betty Crocker. In addition to her artistic accomplishments, McMein also marched in suffrage parades and fought for women's rights. She was inducted into the Society of Illustrators' Hall of Fame in 1984.

HERB RYMAN

PORTRAIT AND CONCEPT DRAWING OF SHARON

WALT COMMISSIONED PORTRAITS FOR BOTH HIS DAUGHTERS when they celebrated their sixteenth birthdays. For his youngest daughter Sharon's portrait, he commissioned Disney Studios artist Herb Ryman. Ryman started his Disney career in 1938 after Walt saw a gallery exhibition of his work. It would be in 1953 that Walt would ask Herb to sketch some of his earliest dreams of Disneyland.

Ryman was a prolific artist outside of his work for Disney, specializing in pen and ink, oil paintings, and watercolor paintings that were sought after by art collectors around the country. According to Ryman, "I was working as an animation director at the studio when Walt took me aside one day and asked for a personal favor. Would I paint a portrait of his daughter Sharon for her sixteenth birthday?"

Today, the artwork hangs proudly in Sharon's youngest daughter Michelle's home. Michelle shared about the portrait: "When I look at [this] painting of my mother in her beautiful red gown I think 'WOW' she was so beautiful and regal. I also see a hint of mischief in it. Maybe I'm reading into it, but she had a bit of mischief in her. I knew her as Mom, and she was the very best at that. Her dedication to her children was unending. She had a lot of different parts to her, mother, philanthropist, board member, jokester, and loyal friend. She had grace and humility. That was Sharon D. Lund."

BELOW LEFT Herb Ryman, *Sharon Disney*, 1952; oil on canvas

BELOW RIGHT Herb Ryman, *Sherry* (Sharon Disney), 1952; pencil on paper

OPPOSITE Neysa McMein, *Diane Disney*, 1949; oil on canvas

THOMAS HART BENTON
LITHOGRAPH COLLECTION

BELOW LEFT Thomas Hart Benton, *Missouri Musicians*, 1933; ink on paper

BELOW RIGHT Thomas Hart Benton, *Wreck of the Old 97*, 1944; ink on paper

OPPOSITE Peter Ellenshaw, untitled painting of a Palm Springs desert landscape, 1965; oil on canvas

THOMAS HART BENTON was an American painter and muralist. Along with Grant Wood and John Steuart Curry, he was at the forefront of the Regionalist art movement. The fluid, sculpted figures in Benton's paintings showed everyday people in scenes of life in the United States. His style was highly influential at The Walt Disney Studios and can be seen visually referenced on screen in such films as *Song of the South* (1946) and the "Johnny Appleseed" segment of *Melody Time* (1948). These works, *Missouri Musicians* and *Wreck of the Old 97* were acquired by Walt and were part of his personal art collection.

Walt and Benton both grew up in Kansas City, Missouri, and were born storytellers who shared the ability to draw and a well-developed sense of humor. Walt attended Benton Grammar School in Kansas City, named after Missouri senator Thomas Hart Benton, the artist's great-great-uncle. Senator Benton was an early nineteenth-century champion of westward expansion and overland trade routes to the Pacific. The artist Benton developed a reputation as an artist of rugged American individualism and for his work reflecting on his family heritage.

PETER ELLENSHAW

PALM SPRINGS OIL PAINTING

WILLIAM "PETER" ELLENSHAW was an English matte artist and special effects creator who worked on many Disney feature films. Born in London, he first worked in matte painting for director and producer Alexander Korda, but his most extensive association was with The Walt Disney Studios, beginning with their first completely live-action feature film, *Treasure Island* (1950). In 1953, he moved to America to continue his work for Walt at the Disney Studios in Burbank, California. He won an Academy Award® for *Mary Poppins* (1964) and retired after his work on *The Black Hole* (1979). In retirement, he fully explored his passion for fine art painting.

Walt introduced Ellenshaw to the beauty of the desert. Walt owned a vacation home in Palm Springs and spent any weekend he could appreciating the Southern California desert. This special artwork depicting the desolate landscape of Palm Springs was part of Walt and Lillian Disney's personal art collection.

PHIL DIKE
COASTAL WATERCOLOR

ABOVE Phil Dike, *Northern California Coast*, c. 1950; watercolor on paper

OPPOSITE Joshua Meador, *Smoke Tree Ranch*, c. 1950; oil on canvas

PHIL DIKE WAS KNOWN as the intellectual and artistic leader of the California Water Color Society. He was strongly influenced by modernist painters Georgia O'Keeffe, John Marin, and Charles Burchfield. He studied and later taught at the Chouinard Art Institute as well as further studies in New York and Paris. Many Disney studio artists also trained at Chouinard, and when the school faced financial troubles Walt and Roy O. Disney orchestrated a merger with the Los Angeles Conservatory of Music, incorporating the California Institute for the Arts in 1961. From 1935 to 1945, Dike worked at The Walt Disney Studios, where he taught art and color theory while working on animated films, including *Snow White and the Seven Dwarfs* (1937), *Fantasia* (1940), and *The Three Caballeros* (1945). After World War II, Dike left Disney and returned to teaching and painting full time where he was remembered as a kind and attentive teacher.

This artwork depicting the Northern California coast, a typical subject of Dike's, was part of Walt and Lillian's personal art collection.

JOSHUA MEADOR

SMOKE TREE RANCH OIL PAINTING

JOSHUA MEADOR WAS AN ANIMATOR, special effects artist, and animation director for the Disney Studios. He also proved to be an imaginative filmmaker. In the 1958 *Disneyland* television episode "Tricks of Our Trade," he recreated his role as animation supervisor for the "Rite of Spring" segment of *Fantasia* (1940), developing the technique of using bubbling mud to simulate lava. He animated on most Disney features and numerous shorts of the 1940s and 1950s, including *Dumbo* (1941), *Bambi* (1942), and *Saludos Amigos* (1943); and created animation effects for *Song of the South* (1946). He was a member of the special effects team for *20,000 Leagues Under the Sea* (1954), for which the Disney studio won the Academy Award® for Special Effects.

Meador was also a remarkable landscape artist, known for his palette knife paintings. While still under contract for special projects at Disney, he maintained studios and galleries all over California.

In the early 1930s, Walt began visiting Palm Springs and stayed at Smoke Tree Ranch, a private enclave. Later, he built a vacation home there and would frequently invite artists who worked for his studio to paint the magnificent Southwest scenery. Meador spent a lot of time in the desert and painting landscapes. This piece is one of many of his works from Walt and Lillian's personal art collection.

"Palm Springs was a wonderful escape for our grandparents and for all of us. The home was filled with a variety of art representing different styles and personalities. Dalí in one room, Joshua Meador in another, and statues of African warriors."

—TAMARA MILLER,
GRANDDAUGHTER OF WALT DISNEY

PART 4

ANIMATION

Prior to *Snow White and the Seven Dwarfs* (1937), Walt Disney had never produced a full-length feature film. Up to that point, The Walt Disney Studios had seen great commercial success with Mickey Mouse and critical acclaim with the artistically daring Silly Symphony series. Walt was eager to grow his studio and knew he had to continue diversifying. The story of *Snow White and the Seven Dwarfs* was his first choice for moving into features.

Walt once reflected, "Because the animated cartoon comes to life on the screen it belongs in the field of the motion picture. But because it is drawn and painted, it is also one of the graphic arts like painting. As a matter of fact, it is often referred to as the last of the graphic arts." Animation proved to be just the first medium in which Walt Disney would innovate, but certainly not the last.

GUSTAF TENGGREN

SNOW WHITE AND THE SEVEN DWARFS (1937) CONCEPT ART

GUSTAF ADOLF TENGGREN WAS a Swedish children's book illustrator and inspirational sketch artist at the Disney studio from 1936 to 1939. His illustrative style, heavily influenced by the work of John Bauer and Arthur Rackham, contributed to the look of *Snow White and the Seven Dwarfs* (1937) and heavily influenced *Pinocchio* (1940) and other Disney works.

Diane Disney Miller first collected this artwork from Disney art dealer and animation art expert, Howard Lowery. She said, "I was buying art as gifts for my children and grandchildren. ... One of the first pieces I acquired was the very small ... exquisite Gustaf Tenggren concept painting of a terrified Snow White surrounded by logs that appear to her to be alligators."

Recounting how the creative process began, animators Frank Thomas and Ollie Johnston wrote in their book, *Disney Animation: The Illusion of Life*, "Before any actual story work was begun, Walt would look for an artist of unique ability to make some drawings or paintings that would excite everybody. He brought in top illustrators of children's books, such as Gustaf Tenggren, to explore the visual possibilities of a subject. These inspirational sketches started the whole staff thinking." Tenggren contributed not just to the visual development of *Snow White* but also to its poster art, which offered moviegoers their first glimpse of the film.

OPPOSITE Gustaf Tenggren, concept art for *Snow White and the Seven Dwarfs* (1937); paint on paper

ABOVE Academy of Motion Pictures, Special Academy Award for *Snow White and the Seven Dwarfs* (1937), 1939; cast metal with gold plate on wood base

OPPOSITE, FROM TOP Cartier, Dopey from *Snow White and the Seven Dwarfs* (1937) money clip, c. 1938; enamel on gold

Cartier, *Snow White and the Seven Dwarfs* (1937) and *Pinocchio* (1940) charm bracelet, c. 1940s; enamel on gold

Cartier, *Snow White and the Seven Dwarfs* (1937) charm bracelet, c. 1938; enamel on gold

SNOW WHITE AND THE SEVEN DWARFS (1937)

SPECIAL ACADEMY AWARD®

THE MAKING OF *Snow White and the Seven Dwarfs* (1937) was one of the greatest challenges of Walt Disney's career. At the time, no one had ever attempted a film such as Walt had envisioned—a feature-length story told through a carefully crafted brand of character animation—and some industry insiders predicted it would be "Disney's folly." Instead, the finished film achieved enormous worldwide success, and laid the groundwork for even more ambitious projects.

This special award consists of the legendary full-size Oscar® statuette and seven miniature statuettes representing the Seven Dwarfs. Upon its release, *Snow White and the Seven Dwarfs* won both the critical acclaim and box office success of a film worthy of Oscar® consideration. Up until that point, it was the highest-grossing film of all time.

Snow White and the Seven Dwarfs is the only film to have been honored by the Academy in two successive years. The first honor came in the year of the film's release (1937), when it was nominated for Best Music (Scoring). On February 23, 1939, the Academy presented Walt with this special eight-piece Academy Award. The Academy honored *Snow White* as "a significant screen innovation which has charmed millions and pioneered a great new entertainment field for the motion picture cartoon."

SNOW WHITE AND THE SEVEN DWARFS (1937)

CARTIER JEWELRY

IN 1937, Cartier, Inc. partnered with Disney to produce a charm bracelet with the likeness of Snow White and each of the Seven Dwarfs. Photographs of Walt and Lillian at the premiere of *Snow White and the Seven Dwarfs* at the Carthay Circle Theatre in December of 1937, show Lillian wearing a very special bracelet—this Cartier bracelet.

Walt owned a matching Cartier accessory: a money clip, which featured Dopey's likeness. Both the bracelet and the money clip were fashioned from 14-karat gold and enamel. At the time these were some of the most exclusive products from the vast array of merchandise that was created for the film. Time and again, Lillian would wear many similar tributes to Walt's achievements.

Cartier would later design another charm bracelet with the characters of Snow White and Pinocchio featured. Both bracelets were part of Lillian Disney's personal jewelry collection.

PINOCCHIO (1940)

MAQUETTE OF PINOCCHIO

THE SECOND ANIMATED FEATURE to emerge from The Walt Disney Studios was *Pinocchio* (1940). This film maintained the high standard of character animation seen in *Snow White*, along with exceedingly advanced animation effects. *Pinocchio* remains the most lavishly detailed animated feature ever made, and one of the most expensive at the time.

Walt was quoted in *The New York Times* on February 4, 1940, saying, "I think the greatest improvement at our studio has been made in the special effects. ... For the first time in the field of animation audiences will see, in *Pinocchio*, the warm glow of a lighted match against a man's face as he lights his pipe. They will see the Blue Fairy step from a dazzling brilliance of light. They will see the most tremendous whale ever heard of, swimming through the water, his muscles rippling subtly under his blueblack hide."

A maquette is a small-scale sculpture, often used to finalize the concept of a design. These three-dimensional models were used during the development of animated films to help animators visualize characters in different poses from any angle. This Pinocchio maquette was created by The Walt Disney Studios' Character Model Department during the production of the film. The Character Model Department, led by Joe Grant, was established at Walt's suggestion in October 1937 and played an integral role in developing new stories and characters.

Joe Grant recalled after the premiere of *Snow White*, "It was [in] one of those conferences in the hallway, and [Walt's] first question was, 'What are we gonna do for an encore?' And that's where he more or less said, 'Let's do some experimenting, let's do some research and see what we come up with.' Which, the result of that was the [Character] Model Department and *Pinocchio*."

TOP Bob Jones, character model of Monstro from *Pinocchio* (1940); paint on plasticine on wood

BOTTOM Sculpture by Disney Studio Artist painted by Helen Nerbovig McIntosh, character model of Pinocchio; paint, plaster, and metal alloy armature

PINOCCHIO (1940)

MAQUETTE OF MONSTRO

MONSTRO—NAMED AFTER the Portuguese word for "monster"—traces his origins to Chapter 26 of Carlo Collodi's original *The Adventures of Pinocchio,* "The Terrible Dogfish." The Dogfish is described as big as a "mountain" or "larger than a five-story building."

Animating Monstro proved difficult, as the studio needed to convey the smooth movements of a large whale bringing a lot of force to the screen. What made Monstro such a "murderous adversary," according to animator and historian John Canemaker, is his capacity to *feel.* He was bad and he knew it.

The early models created in the Character Model Department were created using plasticine—a non-drying clay—and then cast in plaster with an underlying steel wire armature. This maquette is unusual because it was modeled in plasticine, painted, and distributed without having been cast in plaster. When the object arrived at the museum it was in poor condition: most of the tail was detached, exposing metal rods and internal wood supports. The object has since been conserved in a manner that leaves the original material undisturbed, allowing the viewer to enjoy and appreciate the sculpture in its full form, honoring the artist's aesthetic intent, and acknowledging the piece's important place in the making of *Pinocchio.*

FANTASIA (1940)

SOUVENIR PROGRAM

GYO FUJIKAWA WAS HIRED at The Walt Disney Studios as a promotional artist in 1940. She designed a variety of *Fantasia*-themed consumer products, including books, China, glassware, jewelry, textiles, and this theater program. Unlike many Japanese Americans living on the West Coast—including her parents and brother—Fujikawa avoided internment during World War II and worked in New York City designing licensed merchandise. After the war, Fujikawa went on to a prolific career illustrating and writing more than fifty children's books, including some of the earliest to depict racially integrated groups of characters. She also became one of the first children's book illustrators to receive royalties for their work.

Fujikawa later recalled a conversation with Walt regarding the internment of Japanese Americans: "He said, 'How are you doing? I've been worried about you.' I said, 'I'm doing okay. If people ask me what nationality I am I tell them the truth or give them big lies, like I'm half Chinese and half Japanese, or part Korean, part Chinese, and part Japanese.' He said, 'Why do you have to do that? ... Next time anybody asks you that, just tell them it's none of their business. Besides, you're an American citizen.' He was so right. From that time on I just told everybody I was an American citizen. But he was very concerned about the Japanese Americans that worked at the Studios."

FANTASIA (1940)

ROY FORKUM CONCEPT ART

THIS CONCEPT PAINTING BY ROY FORKUM from "The Pastoral Symphony" segment in the movie *Fantasia* (1940) spans almost fifty inches wide and fourteen inches high. Looking closely, you can see the pool with centaurs and centaurettes bathing together. In the foreground there are exotic birds and elaborate detailed trees. In the background you can see Mt. Olympus.

Concept paintings like this were used to convey a visual representation of an idea for a scene. This artwork was most likely used in the process of selecting a color palette for the film segment. According to the Conservation Team at The Walt Disney Family Museum, the shape of the board and numerous marginal notations are evidence that the painting was likely used in the multiplane camera to film and test some of the opening scenes for this sequence. It was discovered upon inspection of this artwork that this is an oil painting over a photograph. This shows us part of the creative process Forkum used to achieve this beautiful piece.

OPPOSITE TOP Gyo Fujikawa (cover illustrator), souvenir program for *Fantasia* (1940); printed ink on paper

BOTTOM LEFT AND RIGHT Roy Forkum, "The Pastoral Symphony" concept paintings for *Fantasia* (1940); oil paint on gelatin silver print

FANTASIA (1940)

KAY NIELSEN CONCEPT ART

KAY NIELSEN WAS A DANISH ILLUSTRATOR popular in the early twentieth century, the "golden age of illustration." He collaborated often with Disney, first contributing story sketches and illustrations for a proposed film biography of Hans Christian Andersen, and then on the "Night on Bald Mountain" and "Ave Maria" sequence of *Fantasia* (1940) before his return to Denmark. During the late 1930s and very early 1940s, Nielsen created story sketches for an unproduced Disney studio version of Andersen's "The Little Mermaid" story that would ultimately help to inspire the production of Disney's 1989 animated feature.

In this concept art, he captures the ferocity of the devil Chernabog who menacingly rules over Bald Mountain. In German folklore, *Sankt Walpurgisnacht*, or Walpurgis Night, was believed to be the night of a witches' meeting on the highest peak in the Harz Mountains. To ward off evil and protect themselves, those who observe the tradition light fires on the hillsides.

BELOW Kay Nielsen, concept art for "Night on Bald Mountain" for *Fantasia* (1940); oil pastel on paper

OPPOSITE Disney Studio Artist, story sketch for *Dumbo* (1941); graphite on paper

DUMBO (1941)
STORY SKETCH

MINDFUL OF THE FINANCIAL LOSSES OF *PINOCCHIO* (1940) and *Fantasia* (1940), Walt gambled on a different type of animated feature. *Dumbo* (1941) was not as complex as the Disney features that came before, but it was even more effective in emotional impact. Animator Ward Kimball recalled the film's origins, saying, "The first time I heard about the story, Walt stopped me in the parking lot and he said, 'Ward, I want to get you started on our next picture. It's a circus picture. It's called *Dumbo,* and it's about a little baby elephant that's born with big ears. Everybody ridicules him.' He went through the whole story in about five minutes."

By the time the holidays approached, *Dumbo* was a financial success. The picture struck a chord with audiences who, in the shadow of World War II, embraced the simple sentiment and inspiring story of a plucky pachyderm and his triumph over adversity.

Dumbo had been planned to be on the December 29, 1941, *TIME* magazine cover as "Mammal of the Year," but then in the early morning of Sunday, December 7, 1941, the attack on Pearl Harbor sent the United States into World War II. Dumbo's cover on December 29, 1941, was replaced with an image of General Douglas MacArthur, noted as "MacArthur of the Philippines." However, *Dumbo* was still featured in the issue in the "Cinema" section. Readers found an unusually candid behind-the-scenes story and loving appreciation of Dumbo, still under the headline "Mammal of the Year," but with an article that had been recrafted to the context of the times.

When *Dumbo* aired during the *Disneyland* television series, Walt said, "From the very start, *Dumbo* was a happy picture. It really started from a very simple idea and ... just grew. We weren't restricted by any set storyline, so we could give our imaginations full play."

BAMBI (1942)

TYRUS WONG CONCEPT ART

CHINESE AMERICAN ARTIST TYRUS WONG started at the Disney Studios in 1938 and when he heard Disney's next feature-length film was to be *Bambi,* he read the book and made sample sketches. These sketches were of lush mountain and forest settings, inspired by Sung dynasty landscape paintings. Wong explained, "I tried to keep the thing very, very simple and create the atmosphere, the feeling of the forest."

ABOVE Tyrus Wong, concept art for *Bambi* (1942); watercolor and graphite on paper

Bringing to life the lush background of the forest proved to be a challenge. According to animators Frank Thomas and Ollie Johnston from their book, *Walt Disney's Bambi: The Story and the Film*, they noted: "Many of the backgrounds we were seeing at this time were

very detailed, almost to the point of looking like photographs, and we were having a serious problem with the unbroken expanse of flat color on the animated adult deer against such paintings." The solution came from Tyrus Wong. "His grasses were a shadowy refuge with just a few streaks of the actual blades; his thickets were soft suggestions of deep woods and patches of light that brought out the rich detail in the trunk of a tree or a log. ... An ethereal quality was there. Best of all, Walt was enthusiastic. 'I like that indefinite effect in the background—it's effective. I like it better than a bunch of junk behind them.'"

BAMBI (1942)

RETTA SCOTT STORY SKETCHES

RIGHT Retta Scott, story sketches for *Bambi* (1942); charcoal on paper

OPPOSITE Mel Shaw, visual development for *Bambi* (1942); pastel on paper

RETTA SCOTT WAS THE FIRST female animator given a screen credit in a Disney film. Scott started working at the Studios in 1939 in the Story Department on *Bambi* (1942). She joined fellow artists like Mel Shaw and Marc Davis in field trips to the zoo, applying her passion for drawing animals. Almost immediately, her charcoal sketches of the powerful sequence where Bambi faces a pack of hunting dogs caught the attention of Walt and the production team. As Frank Thomas and Ollie Johnston later described, "A startling moment for us came when we saw Retta Scott's amazing sketches of the vicious dogs."

Under legendary animator Eric Larson's tutelage, Scott animated the scene of dogs chasing Bambi for the film. Her work demonstrates a mastery of staging, lighting, and camera placement. She described her work, noting, "My director, Eric Larson, gave me much encouragement and guidance. As I only have been working on the dogs, Eric felt that I should clean them up where needed. I estimated that during that year I had drawn over 56,000 dogs for *Bambi*."

BAMBI (1942)

MEL SHAW CONCEPT ART

MEL SHAW JOINED THE *BAMBI* (1942) TEAM as a story and conceptual artist. He contributed to the development of key scenes, offering his talents to envision—among other things—the memorable rainstorm sequence. He produced an exquisite array of pastel, ink, and watercolor studies for the film. These pieces were often impressionistic and full of possibility for animated adaptation. This pastel drawing of Bambi and an owl contrast on the black paper, giving a glowing appearance.

"I think the best education I ever had was during that particular period of time," Shaw said about this period at the Studios, "because of the type of artists that were coming into the studio." On *Bambi*, Shaw befriended and worked with legendary artists like Marc Davis and Retta Scott and enjoyed their zoo field trips where they developed their skills at portraying animals. "I still had a little bit of the old cartoon in my drawings," Shaw recalled. "But they became more refined as the people who were working on it were learning more about animal drawing."

THE ADVENTURES OF ICHABOD AND MR. TOAD (1949)

DICK KELSEY STORY SKETCHES

Dick Kelsey, story sketches for the "Wind in the Willows" segment of *The Adventures of Ichabod and Mr. Toad* (1950); conté crayon and pastel on board

THIS SERIES OF CONCEPT ART STORY PANELS by Dick Kelsey was created for the "Wind in the Willows," segment of *The Adventures of Ichabod and Mr. Toad* (1949), one of the package features released by the Disney Studios after the war. Kelsey, a lesser-known artist who joined the Studios during the boom of the late 1930s, had once been art mentor to master animator Ward Kimball. As essayist Vincent Randle describes, "The style [Kelsey] brought to The Walt Disney Studios was that of fine art, which happened to be the exact flair with which Walt Disney desired to imbue his animated features."

Kelsey's studies are atmospheric, depicting a moody London cityscape on the night of Mr. Toad's escape from prison. Almost entirely in black and white, the staging is cinematic and provocative. In one scene, the shadows cast from Toad's prison cell bars are almost something out of film noir. The sequence in the film was inspired by these concepts, along with two lighter drawings of Toad's new airplane-crazed mania that ends the story.

Though Kelsey's work remains relatively unsung, he holds a special place in Disney history as one of the first artists whom Walt personally recruited to draft concepts for the project that would ultimately become Disneyland.

ABOVE Mary Blair, concept art for *Peter Pan* (1953); opaque watercolor on paper

OPPOSITE, CLOCKWISE FROM BOTTOM LEFT Mary Blair, concept art for *Cinderella* (1950); opaque watercolor on paper board; Mary Blair, concept art for *Cinderella* (1951); opaque watercolor on paper board; Mary Blair, concept art for *Alice in Wonderland* (1951); opaque watercolor on paper; Mary Blair, concept art for *Alice in Wonderland* (1951); opaque watercolor on paper board

A NEW ERA IN ANIMATION

MARY BLAIR CONCEPT ART

MARY BROWNE ROBINSON BLAIR WORKED for Iwerks' animation studio and then at Harman-Ising cartoon productions in the late 1930s before moving to the Disney Studios in April of 1940. Blair's striking use of color and stylized graphics greatly influenced many Disney postwar productions, including: *The Adventures of Ichabod and Mr. Toad* (1949), *Cinderella* (1950), *Alice in Wonderland* (1951), and *Peter Pan* (1953).

For *Cinderella*, Blair was called upon to develop color schemes and staging for nearly every important sequence in the film. Her concepts included designs for the characters, costumes, backgrounds, and a dream sequence in which Cinderella commands an army of her own housemaids.

Walt famously struggled with *Alice in Wonderland* for many years. However, Blair's distinctive style shone through her exploratory paintings. The whimsical and ethereal nature of the bizarre and dreamlike story was very much in line with her unique sensibility, and it gave her the room she needed to flex her creative muscles and conceptualize the strange yet beautiful world of Wonderland.

While it was rare that any of her final designs made their way into the films, her work was used as a creative framing and reference point for the many artists working at the Studios, and Mary Blair admirers can easily spot her color sense and influence in many Disney films.

TULGEY
WOOD
THIS
WAY

MARGARET KERRY'S

TINKER BELL BALLET SLIPPERS

BELOW Capezio, Margaret Kerry's Tinker Bell ballet slippers used during the production of *Peter Pan* (1953); leather and cotton

OPPOSITE Disney Studio Artist, concept art for *Peter Pan* (1953) c. 1939; ink, watercolor, and graphite on paperboard

TINKER BELL IS ONE OF THE MOST ICONIC CHARACTERS to emerge from Walt Disney's legacy, and behind every great character was real-life inspiration. Some of that inspiration came in the form of Margaret Kerry, who served as a live-action reference model for Tinker Bell for animator Marc Davis.

In her donation letter to The Walt Disney Family Museum, Margaret Kerry says of the slippers: "Dancing was a major part of my life from the age of four, starting with lessons with the great Willie Covan, my first tap teacher. He suggested that I should also take ballet lessons. That was why I had ballet slippers. Marc Davis asked me to bring them for the second day of filming on Stage 1 at the Disney Studios. I worked off and on for about nine months. On each day we filmed, I would work in ballet slippers, either my pink or black ones."

PETER PAN (1953)
CONCEPT ART

PETER PAN, A CHARACTER CREATED by playwright and novelist J. M. Barrie in 1902, captivated the imagination of Walt Disney from an early age. Walt saw stage actress Maude Adams portray Peter in the play, *Peter Pan or The Boy Who Wouldn't Grow Up*, in Marceline, Missouri. Later in his career, Walt recalled, "I took many memories away from the theater with me, but most thrilling of all was the vision of Peter flying through the air." Walt was inspired and later performed the role of Peter in a school play.

As early as 1935, Walt looked into acquiring the rights to Barrie's *Peter Pan*. Before the acquisition, Walt assigned artists like Albert Hurter, Bianca Majolie, and David Hall to develop concept drawings. In 1939, the film rights were finalized. After being shelved for nearly a decade due to the Disney Studios' involvement in World War II, production officially began in earnest after the war, and Walt once again turned his attention to *Peter Pan*.

"The greatest challenge I have ever faced is the task—the very pleasurable task—of bringing *Peter Pan* to life," Walt shared during production. "I have been considering *Peter Pan* as a special project almost from the beginning of our feature-length cartoon production. ... It simply had to be made in the medium best suited to its wondrous nature."

SLEEPING BEAUTY (1959)

EYVIND EARLE CONCEPT ART

BY THE TIME HE ARRIVED AT DISNEY IN 1951, Eyvind Earle was already a well-established fine artist. But he was eager to prove himself in animation. Early on in his time at the Studios, Earle found inspiration. As he recalled in his book, *Horizon Bound on a Bicycle,* "I remember the first day I came to work ... up on the wall ... were about 100 exquisite little paintings by Mary Blair. ... I said to myself, 'That's the job I want at Disney.'"

Earle worked as a background artist and would eventually be chosen by Walt Disney to style and paint all the key backgrounds for *Sleeping Beauty* (1959). He also had been granted decision-making power over character designs and color schemes. In essence, Earle was

given control over the film's visual appearance. Walt envisioned a film with a consistent visual style from beginning to end, and he knew that having one artist responsible for the style would achieve the goal—an unprecedented decision at the time.

Earle drew on a variety of artistic styles in his research for *Sleeping Beauty*. He cited his artistic inspirations for the film: Northern Renaissance artists Jan van Eyck and Pieter Bruegel, German Renaissance and Gothic artist Albrecht Dürer, and Italian Renaissance painter Sandro Botticelli. "On top of all that I injected a little piece of Eyvind Earle," he said. *Sleeping Beauty*'s style was a fusion of old and new, and was most certainly distinct.

Eyvind Earle, concept art for *Sleeping Beauty* (1959); acrylic on board

LADY AND THE TRAMP (1955)

WALT'S SCRIPT NOTES

WALT WROTE THIS EIGHT-PAGE SCRIPT OUTLINE for the story of *Lady and the Tramp* (1955). These script notes include character descriptions and various story beats for the film. Walt wrote, "The rat should be planted as enemy of Lady early in the story. He can be [the] gangster type—a real menace—Lady chases him out of the yard every time he appears. Lady is bodyguard for whole family. She thinks herself damn important."

In 1943, Walt bought the story from Ward Greene, a friend and head of King Features Syndicate, which distributed Disney comic strips. Set in an unnamed Midwestern town in the early twentieth century, the movie begins with the words of humorist Josh Billings: "In the whole history of the world there is but one thing that money cannot buy ... to wit—the wag of a dog's tail." *Lady and the Tramp* vividly depicts dogs running around in a lively world from an animal perspective. It was the first Disney animated feature film based on a mostly original story and gave the main characters humanlike personalities with dog movements.

LADIES FAITH IN FAMILY IS STRONG — HER BOY FRIENDS ATTITUDE DISGUSTS HER BUT PLANTS THINGS IN HER MIND THAT LATER EVENTS CAUSE HER TO MISUNDERSTAND

LADY BELIEVES IN PEOPLE — HER BOY FRIEND IS A SKEPTIC

RIGHT Synopsis script notes for *Lady and the Tramp* (1955), c. 1944; graphite on paper

OPPOSITE Milt Kahl, animation drawing for *The Jungle Book* (1967); graphite on paper

THE JUNGLE BOOK (1967)

MILT KAHL CHARACTER DRAWING

WALT DISNEY'S SUDDEN DEATH in 1966 marked the end of an era, leaving the Studios suddenly without its determined and innovative leader.

Since 1962, Walt and the Animation Department had been working on their nineteenth animated feature film, *The Jungle Book* (1967), a musical comedy loosely based on the 1894 Rudyard Kipling book of the same name. Walt's passing led to uncertainty at the Studios, temporarily halting production of the film as employees became concerned about the future of animated filmmaking and management briefly considered shutting down the Animation Department to rely on income from rereleases. Nevertheless, the film was completed and released in 1967, nearly a year after Walt's passing–making it the last animated feature that he personally oversaw. Everything Walt had learned in nearly thirty years of filmmaking was poured into the project: unique character personalities, sight gags, catchy music, and rich background art.

Upon its release, the tremendous success of *The Jungle Book* reaffirmed animation as a valuable form of storytelling, while also reassuring the Animation Department staff that they would be able to move forward without their ambitious leader.

PART 5
INNOVATION

During Walt's lifetime, The Walt Disney Studios was bursting at the seams with creative and technological innovation. Walt pushed his employees to innovate in all areas of filmmaking, resulting in developments that included new techniques to use the Technicolor three-strip process to add color to animated projects, depth in animation using the multiplane camera, and a special optical printer to combine live-action and animation.

"We treat each picture as an experiment. Each unit, or production, has many stages of experimentation," said Walt. "Story construction, scene technique, animation, sound, and color. Throughout these stages we ask ourselves, how can we make it better than good. The wheels of progress run on and on and we want to pull—not push."

Walt shared, "You know I've always had a feeling [that] any time you can ... experiment or do anything, you ought to do it. You'll never know what will come out of it. And I have that feeling today when my boys come to me with an idea and it sounds plausible to me, sounds possible. I try to go with them on the experiment. Because you'll never know what will happen."

STEAMBOAT WILLIE (1928)

UB IWERKS ANIMATION DRAWING

WALT NEEDED TO SELL his new character, Mickey Mouse, and that was much harder with a new character and no big distributor behind you. Ub Iwerks remembered, "Everywhere, [Walt] got the same story: 'Cartoons are dead.' He just could not sell it." Walt knew that he had to do something completely innovative to gain the attention of distributors, theater owners, and the public. *The Jazz Singer* (1927), the first "talking" picture, had recently become a huge hit, and inspiration struck. Walt said, "It occurred to me that in a world gone sound-mad since the release of Al Jolson's *The Jazz Singer*, a cartoon with action synchronized to sound would be something of a sensation. My third Mickey, *Steamboat Willie*, was planned with this in mind."

Steamboat Willie was partially inspired by the successful Buster Keaton comedy, *Steamboat Bill, Jr.* Carl Stalling composed the score for *Steamboat Willie* based on the much earlier and familiar songs "Steamboat Bill" and "Turkey in the Straw." Walt still had to figure out how to synchronize the sound. With help from new sound technology, Walt blew away audiences and critics alike with his revolutionary new synchronized sound.

OPPOSITE
Ub Iwerks, animation drawing for *Steamboat Willie* (1928); graphite on paper

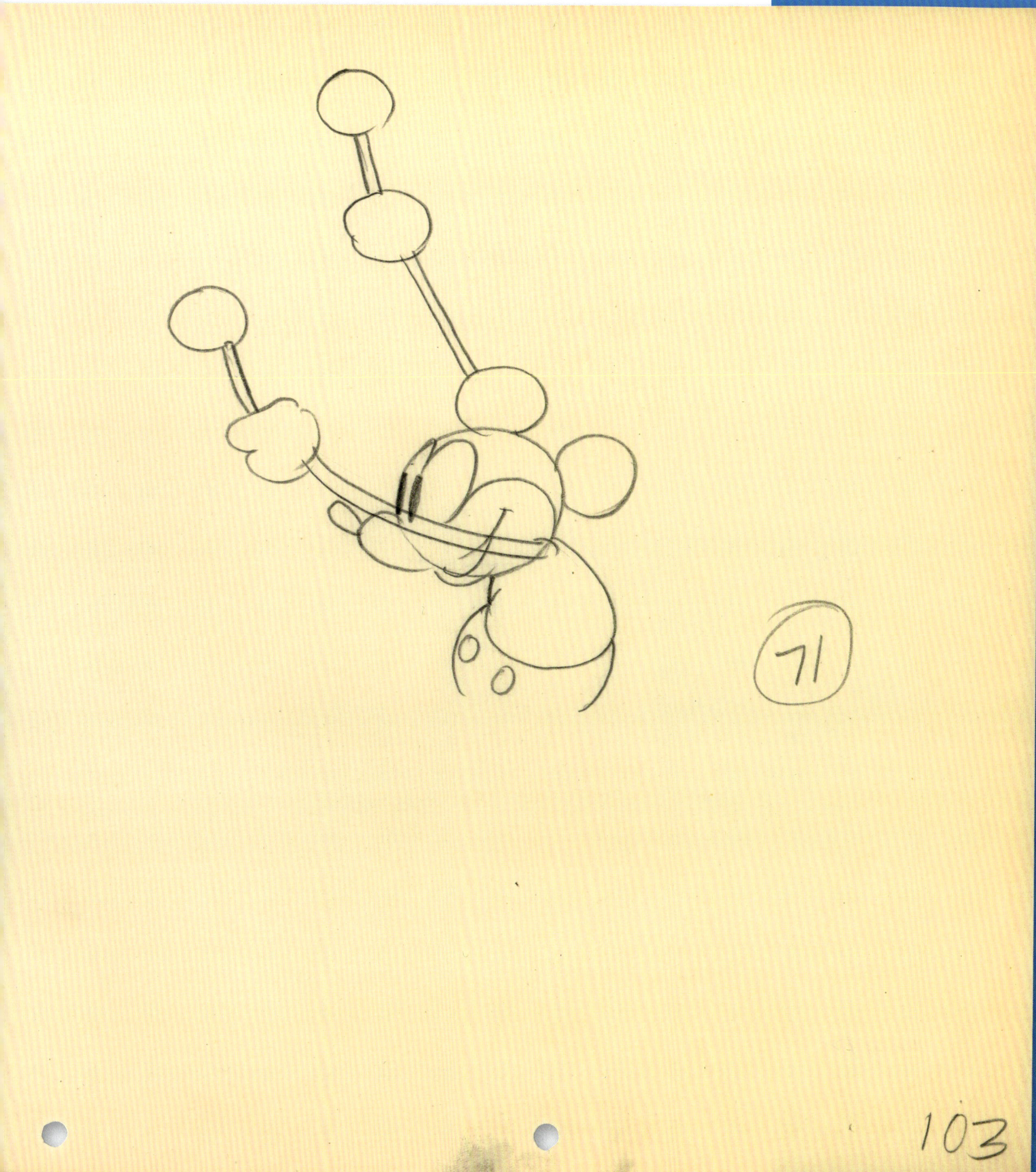
71
103

WALT DISNEY PRODUCTIONS

MICKEY MOUSE MERCHANDISE

BELOW Walt with Mickey Mouse merchandise, c. 1932

OPPOSITE Lionel Manufacturing Company, Mickey Mouse Hand Car, 1934; plastic and metal

***STEAMBOAT WILLIE* WAS AN INCREDIBLE JUMPING-OFF POINT** for Mickey Mouse's success. Cartoons wouldn't be the only avenue available to enjoy Mickey, either. Many first experienced Mickey not in a movie theater, but rather through his ubiquitous image on watch faces, toys, games, coloring books, advertisements, and comic strips. Scores of manufacturers reproduced Disney characters on most anything imaginable. The person most responsible for the initial Mickey Mouse product boom of the 1930s was Kay Kamen, merchandising tycoon.

In 1932, Kay Kamen was considered one of the country's preeminent promotion men and he became Walt's exclusive representative for Disney character merchandise. For Walt and Roy, he helped oversee all contract matters with authorized licensees of Disney product, and gave them new ideas for Mickey Mouse merchandise.

Within the first year, Kamen became completely familiar with the business and began issuing licensing to manufacturers for product not covered in previous contracts. Within the first six months, he was able to report record-breaking merchandise sales.

Mickey merchandise provided much-needed cash flow for the Disney Studios as they entered the 1930s. Walt could experiment further with animation, as he was not solely tied to revenue from Mickey Mouse cartoons box office receipts, and used that freedom for other ventures.

LIONEL CORPORATION

MICKEY MOUSE HAND CAR

FOUNDED IN 1900, THE LIONEL CORPORATION had become an innovator in toy train production by the 1930s. But the Great Depression took its toll, and on May 7, 1934, Lionel went into receivership to avoid bankruptcy. Two months later, Lionel and Kamen discussed an idea: a Mickey Mouse and Minnie Mouse wind-up train handcar.

The wind-up handcar was produced and became available in either red or green, running along a circular O-gauge track. Within four months, more than 253,000 sets were sold. Though the sale of the handcars accounted for only 5 percent of Lionel's business during the latter part of 1934, it was because of Mickey's association with the company that other Lionel products were suddenly in demand, and subsequent sales of these toys helped move the company into the black. By December 31, 1934, Lionel paid its debts in full, and the company left receivership the following month. That one dollar toy was credited with saving the company.

"I should think that there would be a big market for MICKEY dolls, toys, and novelties for the coming season and it may not be a bad idea to feel out the possibilities along these lines as these things are also considered very good publicity."

—WALT

Kamen Limited, *The Auto Ride* store display, c. 1935; papier-mâché, paint, wood, metal, and electrical components

KAMEN LIMITED

THE AUTO RIDE STORE DISPLAY

IN 1934, KAY KAMEN PRODUCED a Disney "Christmas Promotion" kit that included several decorative relief panels to be used for in-store displays. *The Auto Ride* stands an impressive five feet tall and seven feet wide. The piece is "animated," with an electromagnetic motor attached to the back of the panel that operates several of the object's movable parts. Originally painted in bright colors, the panel depicts Mickey Mouse, Minnie Mouse, Horace Horsecollar, and Clarabelle Cow riding in a car to London, with Pluto eagerly running alongside.

Due to years of use, *The Auto Ride* arrived at The Walt Disney Family Museum in 2007 in a fragile state. The overall painted surface was actively flaking and lifting away from the papier-mâché support. The entire panel was covered with a varnish that had darkened and yellowed with time. Many of the brightly painted details were obscured, and the piece had an overall uneven, dark, and unpleasant appearance. The Walt Disney Family Museum Conservation Team undertook the task of stabilizing the papier-mâché support and paint, removing the dirt and grime, and reducing the layer of yellowed, darkened varnish. Care was taken to preserve the integrity of the original object and allow the viewer to see it in its most original form.

LONDON

INGERSOLL

MICKEY MOUSE WATCH

THE ICONIC MICKEY MOUSE WATCH is another prime example of early merchandising success for The Walt Disney Company. Arguably the most popular Mickey items ever, sales from this watch are also credited with saving the Ingersoll-Waterbury Company—today known as the Zeon Watch Group. In 1933 the Ingersoll-Waterbury Company was close to bankruptcy when it was given the license to manufacture watches with a certain famous mouse on their faces. In his biography, *Walt Disney: An American Original*, author Bob Thomas notes, "Within weeks, demand for the watches caused the company to raise the number of employees at its Waterbury, Connecticut, plant from three hundred to three thousand. Two and a half million Mickey Mouse watches were sold within two years." A few years later, the popular watch with Mickey's hands pointing out the time was chosen by officials at the 1939 New York World's Fair to be buried in the Fair's official Time Capsule.

CHARLOTTE CLARK

MINNIE MOUSE AND MICKEY MOUSE DOLLS

THE POPULAR MICKEY MOUSE PLUSH DOLL STYLE seen here was fabricated by seamstress Charlotte Clark in 1930. For a time, three to four hundred dolls were produced weekly, but this sizable quantity still could not satisfy the huge demand.

With growing interest in the doll, Walt and Roy signed a contract with George Borgfeldt & Co. of New York to reproduce the dolls and other novelties. The production output was impressive, but Borgfeldt's licensees couldn't reproduce the quality and craftsmanship benchmarked by Clark. The Disney brothers decided on a unique solution: they released the Charlotte Clark doll pattern to the public so that individuals could make their own dolls. Produced by McCall Company of New York, Pattern No. 91 was sold from 1932 through 1939 with great success.

The Minnie Mouse doll here was given to the original donor, Suzanne Hiller Herrick, when she was a small child in the 1930s. It was made by the women of St. Clement's Episcopal Church in Berkeley, California, and is not only significant in the history of the homemade Charlotte Clark dolls but is also a reminder that Minnie Mouse was a star in her own right, from the very beginning.

BELOW LEFT Charlotte Clark-designed Minnie Mouse plush doll from St. Clement's Episcopal Church, Berkeley, CA, c. 1930; fabric

BELOW RIGHT Charlotte Clark, Mickey Mouse plush doll, c. 1930; fabric and metal

OPPOSITE Ingersoll, Mickey Mouse wristwatch with metal Mickey band, c. 1938; metal

"Kay [Kamen] walked in one day and said, 'I don't know how much business you're doing, but I'll guarantee you that much business and give you fifty percent of everything I do over.' We made a deal with him."

—ROY O. DISNEY

OPPOSITE Henri De Vos, Mickey Mouse French carousel figure, 1930; paint, wood, and cast iron

HENRI DE VOS COMPANY

MICKEY MOUSE CAROUSEL FIGURE

THIS LARGE FRENCH CAROUSEL FIGURE, weighing approximately 225 pounds and standing close to five feet tall, is an extremely rare object, originally acquired by Ron and Diane Miller in 2011. Though little is known about the origins of this figure, it's a product of the Henri De Vos Company. Beginning in the early 1930s, the company specialized in creating fairground sculptures throughout Europe. Since children could not sit atop the Mickey Mouse figure like they would a typical carousel horse, it is believed that this Mickey figure originally "pulled" a cart that children could sit in. Ultimately, this type of iron figure was abandoned in favor of more functional structures.

Henri De Vos Company made Disney character figures for carousels in Europe from the early 1930s until 1960.

THE WALT DISNEY STUDIOS

"ICKMAY OUSMAY" COAT OF ARMS

A 1932 ARTICLE IN *MCCALL'S* MAGAZINE reported that a door at The Walt Disney Studios had a shield bearing a fanciful coat of arms with the mystic words "Ickmay Ousmay," which puzzled studio visitors a good deal. But for guests who recalled that Pig Latin was almost universal among children, that translated to "Mickey Mouse."

Thomas Stanley Curtis purchased the original Disney studio buildings on Hyperion Avenue from the Disney brothers in 1943 for his optical company, Thomas S. Curtis Laboratories. When Mr. Curtis passed away in 1964, the family sold the property. His son, Eric, recalls the whimsical Mickey Mouse coat of arms on one of the doors inside the main building. Most of the studio's doors had been painted over, but through the years, "Ickymay Ousmay" was saved from the painter's brush. Eric reported the crest was cut from the door by a co-worker and presented to him prior to the property's sale.

In November 2012, Curtis's sons Eric and Thomas came to The Walt Disney Family Museum to present the Mickey Mouse coat of arms to Diane Disney Miller, so it could be preserved and presented to visitors of the museum.

THE WALT DISNEY STUDIOS

INK & PAINT JARS

BLACK-AND-WHITE CARTOONS were the standard in the 1930s, and little experimentation had been done at the time to bring color to the screen. The murky two-strip color process in use at the time did not meet Walt's standards for attractive presentation. When he found that the Technicolor company had engineered a three-strip color process that reproduced full, brilliant color—albeit more expensive—he negotiated an exclusive window for use in his cartoons. He now needed a short to perfectly showcase it. His answer was already in production.

Walt stopped production on *Flowers and Trees* (1932) and started the inking and painting process over again in color. It was not a smooth process, with weeks of film tests required to refine the color selection. To use the three-strip technique, the cartoon also had to be photographed at Technicolor's own facility.

Ultimately, *Flowers and Trees* accomplished what no cartoon short had done before. It won an Academy Award for Short Subject, in its brand-new "Cartoon" classification—we know this category today as "Best Short Film (Animated)." Walt would win the first eight consecutive years of this category's existence, and ten of its first eleven.

LEFT Ink and paint jars; glass, paint, plastic, graphite, paper, and ink

OPPOSITE Disney Studio Artist, "Ickmay Ousmay" coat of arms from Hyperion Avenue studio site, c. 1930; paint on wood

"If a woman can do the work as well, she is worth as much as a man ... I honestly believe they may eventually contribute something to this business that men never would or could."

—WALT

OPPOSITE Ingeborg Willy, scrapbook; photographs on paper

INGEBORG WILLY

STUDIO SCRAPBOOK

PICTURED HERE IS A SCRAPBOOK PAGE from Ink & Paint and promotional artist Ingeborg Willy showcasing Disney studio life circa 1937.

During World War II, with widespread male enlistment across the country, the Disney Studios had gaps in its labor force that led to the encouragement of talented women to step into different roles. With many of the trained artists enlisted in the military, the Studios was not creating footage quickly enough. A large amount of work was being commissioned by the government, and there was a need for more staff. Ads were placed in local papers: "Do you want a career in art? Walt Disney needs young women who have had training in pen and ink work, now!" With new trainees enlisted at the Studios, many of the skilled female artists were given the opportunity to move into different departments. By March of 1945, eighty-one women were working in the Animation Building as in-betweeners or assistant animators.

When the United States asked women to join the workforce, it was intended to be temporary. However, when the war ended, women were empowered to earn their own wages and enjoy their own personal and financial freedom. The women who stepped into larger roles at the Disney Studios during World War II paved the way for future generations of female artists.

REPOSING IN THE LOUNGE

IRENE SERVING TEA TO THE GIRLS

OUT FOR A SMOKE AFTER TEA

ENTRANCE TO INKING & PAINTING DEPT.

A GOSSIP DURING TEA TIME

MARGE HUDSON & VIRGINIA AINSWORTH

TIME OUT FOR LUNCH

MAIN ENTRANCE TO THE DISNEY STUDIOS

ENTRANCE TO THE SOUND STAGE

ENTRANCE TO ONE OF THE FILM VAULTS

GIRLS PAINTING THE INKED CELLS.

EVA APPEL MIXING COLORS IN PAINTING LAB.

KAY SUMNER READY TO INK THE CELLS.

ABOVE Schuco, Practical Pig, Fifer Pig, and Fiddler Pig wind-up toys from *Three Little Pigs* (1933), c. 1935; felt and painted tin

OPPOSITE Multiplane camera, c. 1937; metal and glass

THREE LITTLE PIGS (1933)

SCHUCO WIND-UP FIGURES

ANOTHER OF WALT'S KEY INNOVATIONS would be advancing character animation to the point where you could have multiple characters with similar appearances be easily distinguishable by their personalities. Walt found his opportunity with *Three Little Pigs* (1933).

Walt shared, "Each one had a different personality. Whether the two gay little pigs had more or less a group personality. The two of them always worked together. We had the sour little pig there. This is what I was trying to do with the cartoon, to bring more personality on the cartoon."

These three toys were manufactured by the Schuco toy company, founded in 1912 in Nuremberg, Germany—popularly known as Germany's toy capital. In 1934, Schuco struck a licensing deal with Disney, allowing them to design toys from the film. When wound up with a metal key, they move and start playing their instruments. Fifer Pig is playing the flute, Fiddler Pig is playing the fiddle, and Practical Pig is playing the drum. Interestingly, in the film, Practical Pig plays the piano, but it was easier to have his character play the drum instead of a piano for the purposes of this toy.

THE WALT DISNEY STUDIOS
MULTIPLANE CAMERA

THE LAST TECHNICAL ADVANCEMENT left to achieve utilizing the Silly Symphony shorts was mastering the illusion of depth. The multiplane camera was invented at the Disney Studios by William "Bill" Garity and his staff. The towering device had a camera placed at the top where up to six glass levels of foreground and middle ground, above background elements are moved toward or away from the camera, achieving the illusion of depth.

The multiplane camera was first used in the Silly Symphonies short, *The Old Mill* (1937). "For a feature I felt like I had to go to a certain feeling of depth and things," Walt shared. "I couldn't just have the flatness. I did an experimental cartoon that would give me a chance to develop a way of getting depth into my paintings. That is what is now called the multiplane camera. Where instead of it being a painting on one plane, we make the painting into several planes and then we can move the camera through the planes and that gives an illusion of depth."

Both *The Old Mill* and the improvement of multiplane technology netted Walt and his studio staff Academy Awards® for the advancements. Walt joked to *TIME* magazine in 1937, "It was always my ambition to own a swell camera, and now ... I got one."

The multiplane camera continued to be used on feature animation at The Walt Disney Studios through *Oliver & Company* (1988). Today, three original multiplane cameras remain, located at The Walt Disney Family Museum, in San Francsico, California; The Walt Disney Studios in Burbank, California; and Walt Disney Studios Park at Disneyland Paris Resort in France.

HERMAN SCHULTHEIS

CAMERA DEPARTMENT PROCESS LAB NOTEBOOK

CREATED BY ENGINEER, PHOTOGRAPHER, AND TECHNICIAN Herman Schultheis, this notebook documented the innovation of visual effects during his tenure at the Disney Studios from 1938 to 1941, when he worked on *Pinocchio* (1940), *Fantasia* (1940), *Dumbo* (1941), and *Bambi* (1942). He kept a detailed journal about the production of these films, focusing primarily on how the special effects were achieved. The notebook contains photographs, diagrams, and written descriptions demonstrating the experimental and collaborative nature of the studio during this period, when it arguably produced some of its most groundbreaking work.

The notebook demonstrates the step-by-step processes over years of hard work and experimentation that resulted in the visual brilliance of the animated films. The astounding growth and creative explosion at Disney during this period are only too evident in the Studios' first few features.

Not too long after leaving The Walt Disney Studios in 1941, Schultheis left the film business and disappeared into the jungles of Guatemala in 1955. The notebook was lost to history until 1990, when Disney art dealer and animation expert Howard Lowery discovered the notebook in a chest of drawers at Schultheis's former Los Angeles residence.

Herman Schultheis, Camera Department Process Lab notebook, 1939; photographs and ink on paper

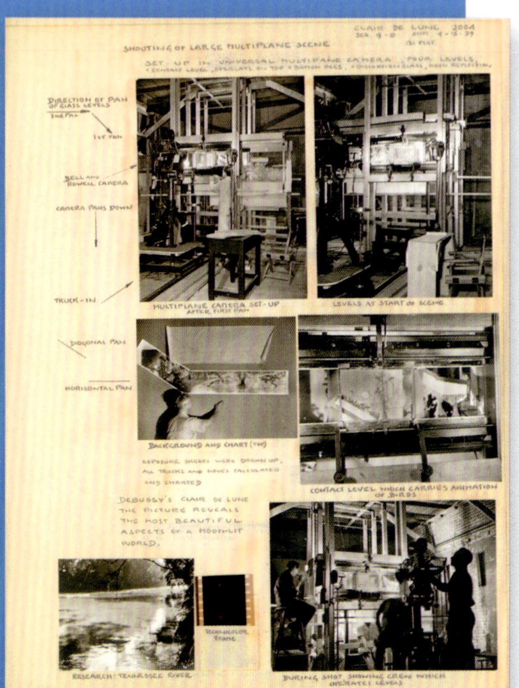

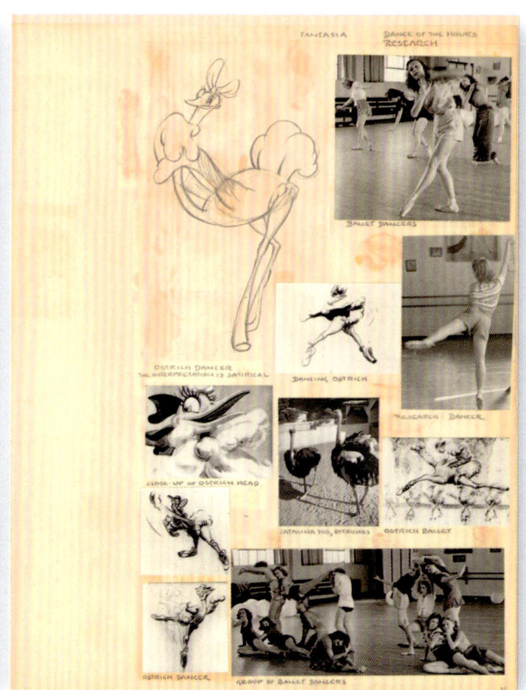

FANTASIA NIGHT ON BALD MOUNTAIN

GHOSTS EMERGING FROM GRAVES

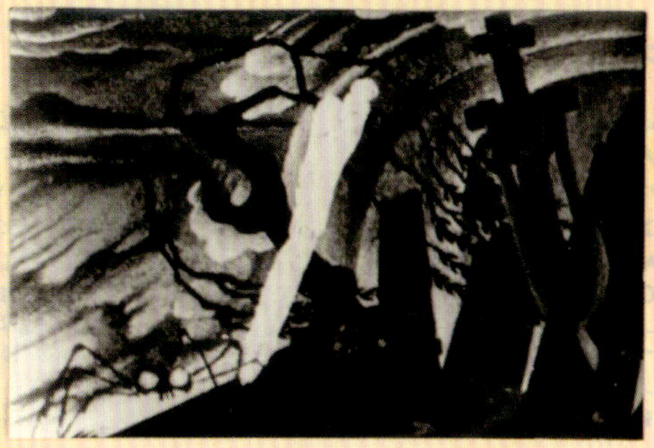

2004 SEQ 11 SC. 27
GHOST OUT OF GRAVE

↙ DRUM ↓ TIN

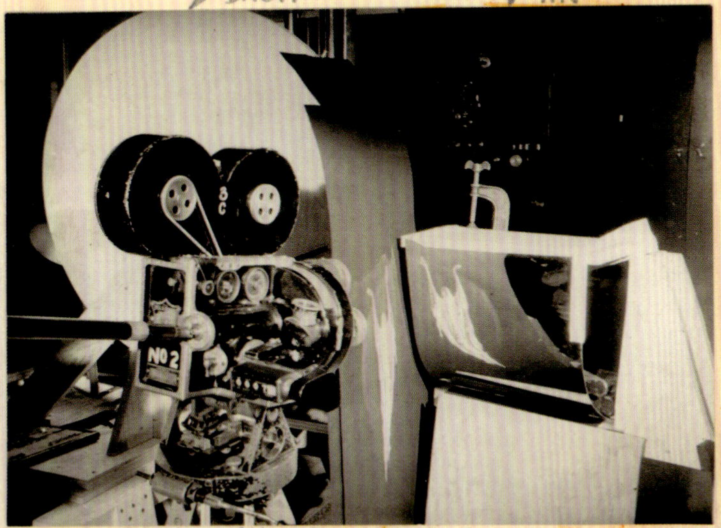

WHITE NEG. GHOST TRAVELS ON OUTSIDE RIM OF DRUM
DISTORTED IMAGE IN THE MIRROR IS SHOT BY CAMERA (BELL + HOWELL)
SPEED OF REVOLVING WHEEL IS GRADUALLY INCREASED TO CAUSE THE GHOST TO DISAPPEAR RAPIDLY

THE GRAVE-STONES ARE ON THE FRONT LEVEL WHILE THE GHOST ARE ON THE BACK LEVELS

LACY GHOSTS EMERGE FROM GRAVES
SHOT ON SMALL MULTIPLANE CAMERA

← IMAGE OF GHOSTS IN MIRROR

← DRAWINGS OF GHOSTS ON BELT

STREAMS OF GHOSTS ON MOUNTAIN

TWO-CELL LAYOUT, BACK LEVEL BEARS BLACK GHOSTS, FRONT LEVEL WHITE GHOSTS

FANTASIA (1940)

JOHN HUBLEY "THE SORCERER'S APPRENTICE" CONCEPT ART

WHEN RECORDING OF *FANTASIA* (1940) BEGAN at the Disney Studios, the limitations of sound equipment at the time did not make the audience feel as if they were really hearing an orchestra perform. Walt assigned his Sound Department to develop a new system that would mimic a concert hall performance. The result was Fantasound, an early surround sound technology.

Fantasound took lots of brainpower and teamwork to pull off. To record the music, William "Bill" Garity—the "technical" mind behind perfecting Disney's multiplane camera—and his team brought literal tons of equipment to the Academy of Music in Philadelphia to capture the Philadelphia Orchestra's performance, even using nine microphones positioned in various locations around the Academy. Nine tracks were recorded, then mixed into three main tracks plus a special notched track. The notched track is key to Fantasound, as it allows the transfer of music to multiple speakers in a specific pattern. This recording was a key pioneer of the surround sound technology we know today.

Due to the expense and number of theaters that could accommodate the equipment, Fantasound was only installed in fourteen theaters around the country—severely limiting the number of patrons who could experience the film the way Walt intended. Walt hoped to exhibit *Fantasia* in concert halls and inaugurate an entirely new form of entertainment, but because of the film's initially disappointing box office results, due to the limited release, and the closure of the European theatrical markets due to the onslaught of World War II, those hopes were quickly scaled down.

RIGHT John Hubley, concept art from "The Sorcerer's Apprentice" from *Fantasia* (1940); watercolor on paper

OPPOSITE Optical Printer, 1943; metal and miscellaneous materials

THE WALT DISNEY STUDIOS

OPTICAL PRINTER #2

BEFORE DIGITAL TECHNOLOGY came into vogue, movie magic in live-action filmmaking was achieved through camera wizardry. How do you film things that don't exist in our world in a way that is believable to the audience? One way is through optical printing, where you can composite multiple reels of film into the same shot. Disney's optical printer was created by animator and inventor extraordinaire, Ub Iwerks.

This device played a major role in Walt's innovative live-action films of the 1950s and 1960s, and continued in earnest post-Walt. This device made it possible to seamlessly weave Peter Ellenshaw's exquisite matte paintings into shots with real sets and live actors, split one Hayley Mills into two sisters for *The Parent Trap* (1961), and enable Bert to dance with penguins in the famous chalk drawing scene from the "Jolly Holiday" sequence in *Mary Poppins* (1964)—among other classic scenes and films. The effects of the latter helped the film garner Walt Disney's only nomination for the Academy Award® for Best Picture.

After years of use, Disney's original Optical Printer #2 was faithfully restored by Don Iwerks for The Walt Disney Family Museum. The display for the Optical Printer is designed to be era specific to when it was used at The Walt Disney Studios.

JOHN HENCH-DESIGNED

1960 WINTER OLYMPIC TORCH

WALT SERVED AS THE CHAIRMAN OF THE PAGEANTRY COMMITTEE for the 1960 Winter Olympics, held in what is now known as Palisades Tahoe in Olympic Valley, California. As chairman, Walt's duties included staging the Opening and Closing Ceremonies, scheduling nightly entertainment for the athletes, providing decorations to enliven the valley, and taking care of a number of logistical details. Walt's son-in-law Ron Miller recalled, "The night before [the ceremonies] it snowed two feet. The athletes couldn't see where they were supposed to march. All of a sudden just as we released the doves ... the sun came out and it was absolutely brilliant. Typical Disney magic."

Veteran Disney artist John Hench even designed the 1960 Winter Olympic torch. Hench's impressive sixty-five-year tenure with Disney spanned positions in the Animation Department, in Special Effects for live-action films, and at WED—now known as Walt Disney Imagineering—working on Disneyland, Walt Disney World, Tokyo Disneyland, Disneyland Paris, and Hong Kong Disneyland. The Olympic Torch is arguably one of his most distinguished design accomplishments.

Though the design was modeled after the torches for the 1948 and 1956 Olympiads, Hench decided on a slightly smaller version that would be easier for torchbearers to carry. The earlier, taller models proved to be difficult to manipulate as they were top-heavy when filled with fuel. Hench also added black tape to the top part of the shaft to enable runners to pass the torch easily and ensure a stable grip. Several subsequent torch designs would be greatly influenced by Hench's 1960 model.

RIGHT TOP Olympic torch presented in Recognition of Preparations for Running of the Flame at the 1960 Winter Olympics in Olympic Valley, 1960; metal on wood

RIGHT BOTTOM Walt and John Hench looking over Olympics plans, 1960

OPPOSITE Walt with grandchildren at the Olympics, left to right: Joanna, Tamara, Walt, and Christopher, 1960

PART 6

CREATIVITY

In 1931, Walt's almost total immersion in his work contributed to what he described as a "nervous breakdown." He had become more irritable with his staff and was often short-tempered. Disappointments could send him into a crying spell, and he suffered from insomnia. When he consulted a doctor, it was recommended he spend time away from the studio and have complete rest. Walt and Lillian took this advice and booked their first nonbusiness trip since their honeymoon five years earlier.

When Walt returned to work, he varied his routine with exercise. He pursued sports like skiing, polo, and lawn bowling. He would often leave work early so he and Lillian could go horseback riding in the hills behind their home in Griffith Park. He found solace and exercised his creativity in building model trains and miniatures, which famously evolved into the assembly of his own backyard-scale railroad. From that came one of many inspiration points for Disneyland Park, and the rest, as they say, is history. While Walt worked incredibly hard for the rest of his life, he made time for his mental health, his hobbies, and his family, and sought a healthier work-life balance wherever he could.

WALT'S MINIATURE COLLECTION

FOR A MAN WHO ALWAYS HAD BIG DREAMS, Walt took some of his greatest delight in the world of miniatures. For decades, he both constructed and collected a huge variety of intricate tiny objects. His collection when cataloged included more than one thousand tiny treasures. In a letter to a friend in 1951, Walt wrote: "My hobby is a life saver. When I work with these small objects, I become so absorbed that the cares of the studio fade away ... at least for a time."

Walt's fascination with miniatures was solidified in 1939, when he saw the famous Thorne Miniature Rooms exhibit at the Golden Gate International Exposition in San Francisco. Using miniature furnishings and accessories, Narcissa Thorne had created exquisite rooms decorated to represent European and American interiors of different eras.

Collecting miniatures wasn't enough, though; he wanted to create miniature worlds, some reflecting specific moments from U.S. history. Walt spent countless hours carefully constructing his tiny tableaus. One diorama, entitled "Granny Cabin," was based on a set from his live-action feature *So Dear to My Heart* (1949). The cabin was exhibited at the Festival of California Living at the Pan Pacific Auditorium in Los Angeles from November 28 to December 7, 1952.

Walt started to develop the idea of a traveling exhibit made up of twenty-four miniature scenes. A press release announced that it represented the beginning of Walt's new miniature Americana exhibit, entitled "Disneylandia." The traveling exhibit concept ultimately proved to be unable to generate the necessary viewership to warrant continued maintenance. The name Disneylandia, however, would grow into something much larger—what is known today as Disneyland.

OPPOSITE Walt with Kathryn Beaumont in front of "Granny Kincaid's Cabin," 1952

Collection of miniature
dining plates; ceramic

Miniature bedroom set; acrylic paint on wood, fabric, metal, yarn, c. 1945

MINIATURE
FOUR-POSTER BED

AMONG WALT'S COLLECTION OF MINIATURES were objects that he collected as well as items that he meticulously constructed himself, part by part, and accessorized beautifully. This four-poster bed is a classic example of the latter.

The linens on the bed stand out—light pink, with orange, yellow, and white flowers behind green and darker pink circles making up the design. According to Diane Disney Miller, Walt created this bedspread and pillow set from Diane's spare fabric. The meticulous design of this set is evident. The bedspread boasts hand-sewn hems on all the edges and the pillow coverings on the open side have frayed edges. The fraying of the edges would have been hand done.

While it can't be said for sure how Walt put this example together, it is fun to imagine how he sourced the fabric from his daughter and sewed the pieces together to customize this bed's look.

MINIATURE
WEDDING CUPBOARD

THIS WEDDING CUPBOARD WALT PURCHASED from his travels in Austria, depicts a replica of an endowment chest that a farmer's bride would be given for her marriage in the eighteenth century.

This ornately decorated cupboard is beautifully hand-painted. It has two doors that open, and it is filled with miniature linens, wool, jewelry tins, a rosary bead necklace, prayer books, an umbrella, a money chest, and a collection of yarn. There is a basket of flowers painted on the top of the cabinet and small details on the right- and left-hand corners are the numbers 18 and 15, indicating the year 1815, to which the cabinet is meant to harken back.

On the back, a description of the miniature has been translated here from German to English; it reads: "This little chest, a special feature of our premiere products, is not a toy, but a showcase display piece. It depicts in exact replication an endowment chest, as the farmer's bride would be given for her marriage in the olden times, with linen, bedding, loden, as well as flax and wool. In the drawer [are] the jewelry tins, prayer books, special bonnet, and various cloths, underneath clothing, umbrella and the money chest."

MINIATURE
BIBLE AND QUR'AN

ALTHOUGH AS AN ADULT Walt did not attend church, he was a man of faith and had a great respect for all religions. Walt and Lillian made a conscious effort not to impose their own religious views on their daughters. Diane Disney Miller shared: "Dad drove us to Sunday School every Sunday for some years. I do know he had great respect for all faiths." When a 1955 Disneyland employee, Earl Anderson, suggested that Walt might consider building a Holy Land amusement park, Walt replied, "I'm a religious man, but here, at Disneyland, we have no religious confinements. All religions are welcome."

"I learned to believe in the basic principle of the right of a man to exercise his faith and thoughts as he chooses," Walt said. "Every person has his own ideas of the act of praying for God's guidance, tolerance, and mercy to fulfill his duties and responsibilities."

It is not surprising to find a miniature Qur'an and a Bible among Walt's collection. There are a few different versions of miniature Bibles in Walt's collection, including the New Testament, and different bindings of the Bible, one dating to 1775.

PENNSYLVANIA PRR 6137

TRAIN MODEL

WALT ACQUIRED THIS N-GAUGE MODEL Pennsylvania PRR 6137 train on July 1, 1955. Walt greatly admired the railroad systems, and recognized how important they were for America's continued growth and prosperity. He was passionate about trains since boyhood. In the October 1965 issue of *Railroad Magazine*, Walt wrote, "I suppose I've always been in love with trains. As a small boy living on a farm near Marceline, Missouri, I had a unique claim to fame: my Uncle Mike was engineer on the Santa Fe's accommodation train that ran between Marceline and Fort Madison. That was something to brag about to my schoolmates at a time when railroads loomed large in the scheme of things and steam engines were formidable and exciting."

He continued, "We fellows would marvel at the tall, stacked engines that pulled into and out of the depot opposite the park where we played, huffing with steam and trailing nebulous smoke plumes. One day in about 1909, when I was eight or nine years old and full of nerve, my buddies dared me to climb into the cab of one of them that stood there, temporarily deserted, and pull the whistle cord. I did so, but as soon as the whistle shrieked, I quickly climbed down in a panic and ran like the dickens."

OPPOSITE TOP Miniature Bible, 1775; metal and printed ink on paper

OPPOSITE BOTTOM Miniature Qur'an with magnifying glass; leather and printed ink on paper

BOTTOM Pennsylvania PRR 6137 model train; metal and wood

THE *LILLY BELLE*

ONE-EIGHTH SCALE TRAIN

NAMED AFTER WALT'S WIFE LILLIAN, the *Lilly Belle* is a one-eighth scale model of an actual steam engine. By comparison, the Disneyland Railroad is five-eighths scale. Walt built the *Lilly Belle* with coaching and assistance from his accomplished studio machine shop team. His eventual backyard right of way, the Carolwood Pacific Railroad, ran around a half-mile track encircling his Holmby Hills home.

He explained in the 1965 issue of *Railroad Magazine*, "After serving an apprenticeship in a machine shop, I studied metalwork and carpentry before I figured I was ready to start building. Then I built a train to one-eighth scale. The engine and the tender combined was seven feet long and operated on coal and water. I fashioned all the cars myself. The boxcars were big enough for a person to straddle, and the flatcars could seat two. My special pride was the caboose, which I furnished entirely in miniature, right down to the potbellied stove. The engine was designed after one that had run on the old Central Pacific, so I named my little railroad the C.P., for Carolwood Pacific, the street I lived on."

This project brought together artists, machinists, and railroad enthusiasts who would go on to be some of his earliest Imagineers. Many animators, friends, and notable people have ridden this train—including artist Salvador Dalí. With the *Lilly Belle*, Walt was able to combine two of his loves: miniatures and trains.

TOP Walt, Diane, Sharon, and guests riding the *Carolwood Pacific*, c. 1950

BOTTOM *Lilly Belle* engine; metal and wood

OPPOSITE LEFT *Lilly Belle* caboose, 1949; metal, wood, and glass

OPPOSITE RIGHT Walt Disney Miniature Stove Works Burbank California, potbellied caboose stove, c. 1949; paint on cast iron

HAND-PAINTED

POTBELLIED STOVE

WALT FASHIONED THE ONE-EIGHTH SCALE potbellied stove to be used in the interior design of the *Lilly Belle* caboose. Walt shared, "I had a pattern made up, and it turned out so cute with the grate, shaker and door, and all the little working parts, I became intrigued with the idea. I had a few made up: one was bronze, another black, and I even made a gold one! Then we made more and started painting them in motifs that fit the period at the turn of the century."

Each of these five and a half inch-tall stoves had a different design, and eventually about one hundred were made. Walt gave some to friends, and even sent some to an antique gift shop in New York where, to Walt's delight, Narcissa Thorne herself purchased two to add to her renowned collection, the same collection that had inspired Walt's hobby. They sold for twenty-five dollars each and Walt made no special effort to market them or make a profit. He was curious to see if there was any interest, and by 1957 the supply was depleted. "It has been fun making them and others appreciate them, too, so all in all, I feel well repaid," said Walt.

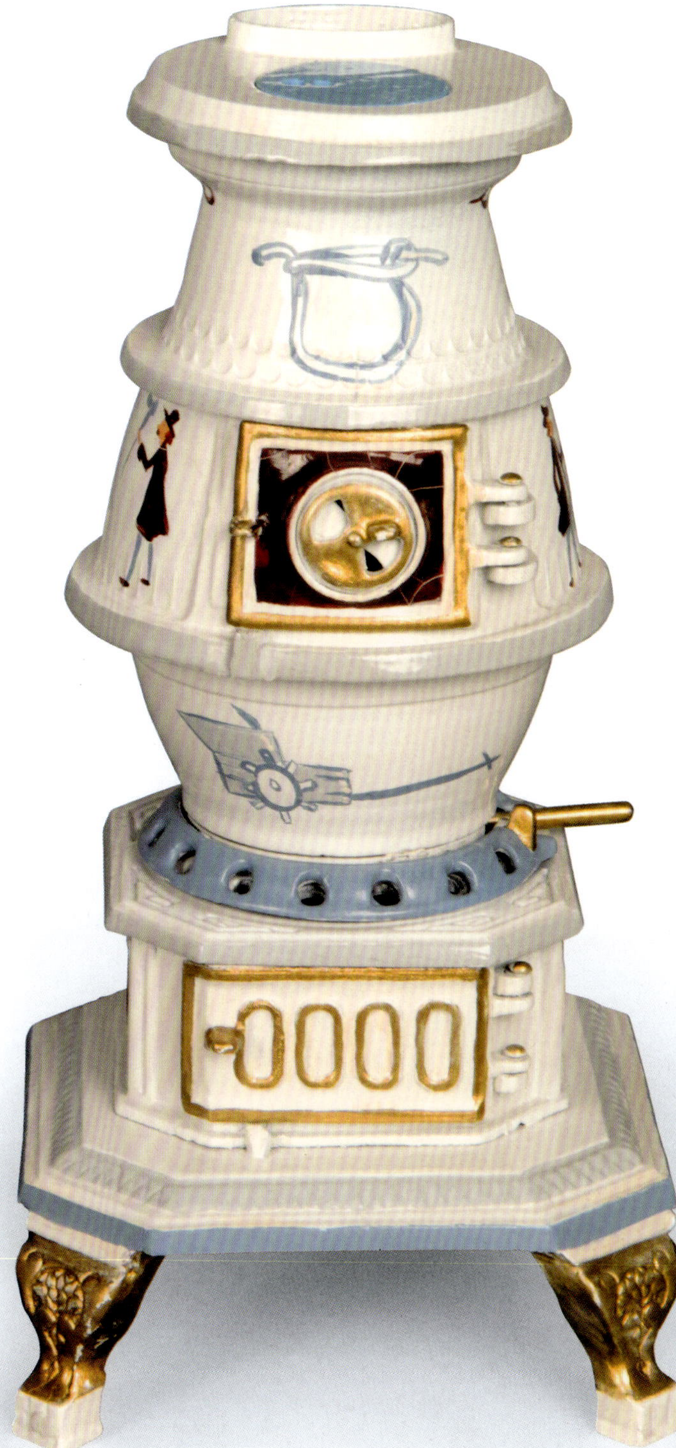

WALT'S
TRAIN UNIFORM AND POCKET WATCH

WALT AND HIS VISITORS enjoyed riding the small-scale Carolwood Pacific Railroad around his home, but he retired it in favor of an even bigger project. "Disneyland Park came along," Walt recalled. "I had the excitement of creating an honest-to-goodness railroad—well, five-eighths scale anyway—the Disneyland and Santa Fe [Railroad]." Whenever Walt was at Disneyland, he was the official chief engineer of the officially named Santa Fe & Disneyland Railroad. Walt kept this pair of overalls in his apartment above the Main Street firehouse so he could change into costume whenever he had time to spare. He'd then tell the on-duty engineer to take a break and would enjoy some "throttle time." Many guests had no idea that Walt Disney himself was operating the train they were riding.

Along with Walt's train uniform, he would carry his antique 1894 American Waltham Watch Company watch. The back of the watch is engraved with an image of a train inlaid with copper. Timekeeping was an important aspect of a conductor's duties. It was crucial if two trains were moving in opposite directions. If one of the two conductors' watches was keeping bad time, there was a strong likelihood of a collision.

"When I was about twelve or so during a visit with my granny at her home, she presented to me my grampa's keepsake box he kept on his bathroom dresser. Inside was a treasure trove of small personal items of my grampa's, including many of his watches. This pocket watch was the largest of the group and I was quite taken with it."

—WALTER MILLER,
GRANDSON OF WALT DISNEY

LEFT American Waltham Watch Company, pocket watch, 1894; porcelain and metal

OPPOSITE Hercules, Walt's train uniform jacket and overalls, c. 1950; cotton, fabric, and metal

WALT'S
COWBOY BOOTS

WALT'S LOVE OF HORSES goes as far back to his time living in Marceline, Missouri, in 1908. Walt's neighbor, Dr. Leighton "Doc" Sherwood, commissioned a seven-year-old Walt to draw a picture of his horse Rupert. As an adult, Walt's love of horses manifested into a lifelong hobby of horseback riding.

The Disney Studios purchased the Golden Oak Ranch in 1959 for Walt to use as a filming location, after he had become familiar with the area while using it as a production location for his "Spin and Marty" television serials. There were a few lucky horses that would go on to retire and live out their days on the ranch. One such lucky horse was Diamond Decorator, better known as Tornado, the black stallion ridden by Zorro in the popular Disney television series.

Walt shared his love of horses with his daughters and grandchildren and the tradition was passed on. Walt's granddaughter Tamara Miller recalls, "My grandfather loved to put on a cowboy hat and boots on occasion, often when we would go to the Golden Oak Ranch, where Tornado, Zorro's horse, was retired along with a stable of other horses and a pony. I was horse crazy, and this was my favorite place."

The Disney love of horses continues. "I raised my children on a ranch raising horses," Tamara shares. "My mother felt it was only fitting to pass the boots on to my son, Ryan. He often says that they are his most prized possession, and I would have to agree."

RIGHT Walt's cowboy boots, c. 1950; leather

OPPOSITE TOP Walt's saddle, c. 1940; silver on leather and wood

OPPOSITE BOTTOM Walt rides a horse at the annual ride of Los Rancheros Visitadores, Santa Barbara, 1939

WALT'S

LOS RANCHEROS VISITADORES SADDLE

WALT WAS A MEMBER of Los Rancheros Visitadores, a group founded in 1930. Every May, the members would meet on the ranchland in Santa Barbara, California. Walt attended for many years. The group would receive a blessing from the Santa Ynez Mission and embark on a sixty-mile horse ride north. This mirrored the trek of cattle ranchers in the mid-nineteenth century who would meet and join together to drive their cattle to market.

According to Diane Disney Miller, "He enjoyed the ride, and the camaraderie. During one of those rides this saddle was won by him through the purchase of a two-dollar raffle ticket." This beautiful, detailed saddle was made by the Stock Saddle Company in San Francisco. Walt never rode on this particular saddle, but he made use of it later as a prop for close-up scenes of Zorro's horse, Tornado.

POLO PARAPHERNALIA

THOUGH ALWAYS ACTIVE as a young adult, Walt didn't participate in sports on a regular basis until the early 1930s, when a doctor recommended that he exercise to relieve stress. Walt played polo, and even started successful teams of players from the studio, one named after Mickey Mouse, and the other after Donald Duck.

Walt's interest in polo also led to a Mickey Mouse cartoon called *Mickey's Polo Team* (1936) in which Disney characters faced off against caricatures of Hollywood's top stars of the day, riding horses that resembled their riders.

This trophy was won by Walt and his team, Buddy Rogers, Dean Morrison, and R.W. Williams on November 21, 1937. They competed at the U.S. Polo Association Pacific Coast Tournament 6 Goal Championship that was held at the Rivera Club in Pacific Palisades, California.

TOP Walt and Reginald "Snowy" Baker playing polo, c. 1932

BOTTOM U.S. Polo Assn. Pacific Coast 6 Goal Tournament Championship cup, 1937, metal

OPPOSITE Walt on a polo pony, c. 1932

UNIVERSITY OF SOUTHERN CALIFORNIA

TROJANEERS LIFE MEMBER CARD

IN 1934, A GROUP OF UNIVERSITY OF SOUTHERN CALIFORNIA (USC) STUDENTS formed the first USC Polo Club. Their very first match was against Walt Disney's Mickey Mouse team, and USC triumphed 7 to 6. According to the January 22, 1934, edition of the *Southern California Daily Trojan*, "Walt Disney was easily the best player on his own team, being continually the center of the battle and very often emerging from the milling ponies and riders with the ball on its way to a score." Walt would score four of the six points.

Walt, who never went to college but received an honorary Master of Science from USC (as well as honorary degrees from several other notable institutions), was a founding member of the Trojaneers Booster Club in 1934 and went on to become its president in 1939. In 1938, he was awarded the University of Southern California Life Member Award.

Walt later explained, "[The Trojaneers are] composed of men who didn't go to college, who give jobs to those who did—athletes particularly." The group originated from a suggestion that Trojan season ticket holders should organize to meet the team and coaches and become better acquainted with the university.

Walt's daughter Diane would later attend USC, where she would meet Ron Miller, a member of the USC football team. They would marry in May 1954.

BELOW Life Member of USC Trojaneers honorary card, 1938; enamel on gold

OPPOSITE Walt's lawn bowling bag and balls; leather, and lignum vitae wood

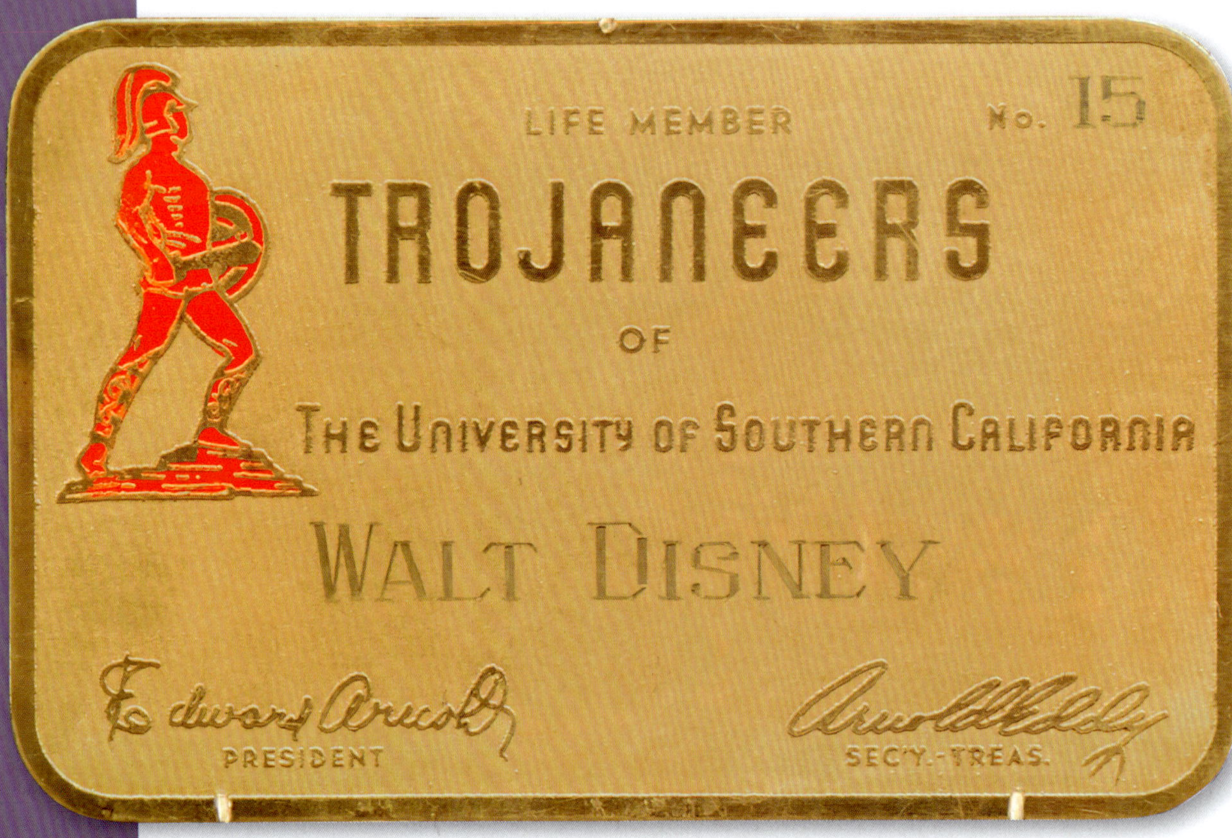

WALT'S
LAWN BOWLING BAG

WALT ENJOYED HIS TIME at Smoke Tree Ranch in Palm Springs. He and Lillian owned a home in the exclusive enclave of privately owned homes on 375 acres of natural desert. There were lots of activities that took place at the Ranch, including horseback riding, which Walt and Lillian would often enjoy on early mornings.

Walt took a particular interest in the Smoke Tree tradition of lawn bowling and became a member of the Smoke Tree Lawn Bowling Club. He would partake alongside the enclave's other lawn bowling enthusiasts and spend entire afternoons rolling lopsided balls across a one-hundred-foot green space.

One of Walt's granddaughters, Jennifer Goff, remembered her time at Smoke Tree Ranch: "It was very low-key, [a] perfect place for him. You'd go down into the clubhouse for dinner, and you'd go into the kitchen for the cafeteria-style meal and Grampa loved it. He'd lawn bowl there. He had quite a few [sets of lawn bowls]. It was just freedom for us, growing up in a big city, you know. He had a bike for every one of us."

WALT'S

ATTENHOFER DOWNHILL SKIS

WALT TOOK UP SKIING in the mid-1930s on skis similar to these Attenhofer downhill skis. Late in that decade, Walt met Austrian Olympic skiing champion Hannes Schroll, who was the head of the Yosemite Ski School. The two became good friends. In 1938, Schroll and his business partners purchased land in the East Sierras, with the intention of building a ski resort near Donner Peak and the small town of Truckee, California.

Schroll had sought financial assistance from Walt in building the resort that eventually became Sugar Bowl Resort in Norden, California. To honor Walt's support and partnership, Schroll changed the name of Hemlock Peak to Mount Disney. The pages of Walt's photo album feature one of Walt's skiing adventures at Sugar Bowl Ski Resort in Northern California, circa 1946.

Among the preeminent enticements that drew skiers to Sugar Bowl in those early years were the chairlift up Mount Disney, the first such lift in California, and the lodge, designed by architect William Wurster and later featured in a Goofy cartoon, *The Art of Skiing* (1941).

Walt vacationed at Sugar Bowl in early 1941 with his family. Of that trip, Diane Disney Miller recalled, "I remember that I very much wanted to learn to ski, and the highlight of the trip was when Hannes took me up the chairlift, with my parents, on Mount Disney and skied down with me on his shoulders."

LEFT AND OPPOSITE Photographs from Sugar Bowl Disney album, c. 1946; photos on cardboard

RIGHT Attenhofer, Walt's skis, c. 1930; metal and leather on hickory wood

WALT'S

KODAK INSTAMATIC CAMERA

THE KODAK INSTAMATIC 804 was produced in 1965 and was an update to the Instamatic 800. This became Kodak's top model for the line of 126 film cartridge models. This model adopted the then-new flashcubes, which rotated as the film was wound to bring the next unused bulb to the front.

Walt brought his Kodak Instamatic camera with him on many of his final family trips, including a trip with his grandkids to San Diego and a family trip to Vancouver. Walt's granddaughter Tamara shared, "I remember him with a camera and possibly the cutest thing about him with his camera, [he] want[ed] a child to snap pictures of him and somebody else. He'd have to crouch down ... instead of asking the child—whoever it would have been—to point the camera up toward him. ... He was constantly crouching to get himself in the vision of the camera."

TOP Kodak Instamatic Camera 804, 1965; paint on metal and plastic

BOTTOM Walt sitting on a patio in Kaua'i, Hawaii, on-location for principal shooting of *Lt. Robin Crusoe, U.S.N,* 1965

OPPOSITE 16mm Bell & Howell 200 Electric Eye movie camera, c. 1957; metal, leather, and glass

WALT'S

BELL & HOWELL MOVIE CAMERA

THIS BELL & HOWELL 200 ELECTRIC EYE 16MM MOVIE CAMERA was described in its user manual as, "It assures you of pictures having superb quality" and "It embodies the ultimate in operating simplicity." The 200 Electric Eye (200EE) was originally produced in 1957 and sold for nearly three hundred dollars and was not the first Bell & Howell camera Walt owned. But rather than the much earlier 2709 Standard Cinemachinery model he used to film the live-action scenes for the Alice Comedies, Walt used this 200EE movie camera to document his travels with his family.

Walt took this camera to document memories on his final family trip to Vancouver. During this trip, the family celebrated Walt and Lillian's anniversary and their granddaughter, Tamara's, birthday. "That Vancouver trip was wonderful," Tamara recalls. "I just remember it being a very happy time for all of us kids and for my parents. I think at that time we must have been somewhat shielded from the fact that he was very ill, because those aren't what my memories were about. We would stop at a lot of different beaches, walk through the woods, the beautiful British Columbia area."

PART 7
IMAGINATION

As he later acknowledged, Walt Disney dreamed up the concept for Disneyland while sitting on a bench near the Merry-Go-Round at Griffith Park in Los Angeles, California. From there, Walt's imagination sparked an entirely new venture, creating theme park entertainment. Walt would sit on the bench eating peanuts, watching his daughters having fun, thinking to himself that there should be an amusement enterprise where the whole family can share in the fun. Walt's daydream eventually coalesced into Disneyland Park and opened a prolific chapter in both his life and pop culture history.

He envisioned the Park as a gift that would keep on giving for generations to come. As he explained to a journalist in 1965: "The park will never be finished. It's something I can keep improving every year. I've always wanted to work on something that keeps growing. I have that now. Disneyland will never be completed as long as there is imagination left in the world." Walt's words proved to be true even long after his untimely death. And his imagination didn't stop with Disneyland.

ORIGINAL
GRIFFITH PARK BENCH

IN ADDITION TO DRIVING HIS DAUGHTERS Diane and Sharon to school every day until they were of driving age, Saturdays were "Daddy's Day," and included regular trips to Griffith Park to ride the merry-go-round. Walt remembered, "[Disneyland] came about when my daughters were very young and Saturday was always Daddy's Day. ... I'd take them to the merry-go-round ... and as I'd ... sit on a bench ... I felt that there should be something built ... where the parents and the children could have fun together. So that's how Disneyland started. ... But it all started from a daddy with two daughters wondering where he could take them where he could have a little fun with them, too."

This bench is original to Griffith Park, where Walt conceived of Disneyland. This was gifted to Diane Disney Miller by Griffith Park during a renovation of the park. Another of the Griffith Park benches is located in Disneyland in the Opera House lobby.

DISNEYLAND
TICKET BOOK

IN THE EARLY DAYS AT DISNEYLAND, Guests paid admission to the Park, and would purchase an individual ticket every time they would like to experience an attraction. On October 11, 1955, Disneyland debuted the first ticket book. For just $2.50 per adult, $2.00 per junior, and $1.50 per child, ticket books included admission to the park and a selection of A, B, and C tickets for eight attractions. The D ticket was added in 1956 and the famous E ticket was added in 1959 for the most sophisticated attractions. The implementation of the ticket book completely changed how Guests experienced the park. The term "an E ticket ride" would become synonymous with an exhilarating experience.

Ticket books were discontinued in June 1982 and replaced with passports that allowed admission and unlimited access to park attractions, which is how Disneyland is experienced today.

ABOVE Disneyland ticket book, c. 1959; printed ink on paper

LEFT Griffith Park bench, c. 1940; wood on metal

Peter Pan
Enjoy the exciting adventures of
SNOW WHITE
PETER PAN
MR. TOAD
Fantasyland

TOMORR

DISNEYLAND
ATTRACTION POSTERS

AS GUESTS ENTERED DISNEYLAND they were met with a tantalizing glimpse of the adventures ahead. They could see the Main Street Train Station that sat above the floral Mickey Mouse icon. Attraction posters lined the fences and advertised what they could explore while visiting Disneyland. They would then travel through tunnels and enter the park as if it were the opening act of the film, stepping onto Main Street, U.S.A.

Walt Disney Imagineering creative executive Marty Sklar shared, "A lot of the posters were colorful and beautiful to look at, gave people directions, and an understanding of what was in the Park."

Bjørn Aronsen (commonly spelled Aronson) created the early attraction posters in 1955 and 1956. These were large, silk-screened graphics that were consistent in style and theme that represented the lands—Adventureland, Frontierland, Fantasyland, and Tomorrowland. The printing technique aided in the effectiveness of these posters, making them attention grabbing with stark colors and graphics.

Some of the first posters to be placed at the entrance were *Autopia, Jungle Cruise, Rocket to the Moon*, and *Santa Fe & Disneyland Railroad.* Imagineer Tony Baxter shared, "Walt didn't want Guests to rest for a minute. Right in the middle of the Tomorrowland concourse would be posters for attractions in other lands. So when Guests exit *Space Station X-1* or *Rocket to the Moon*, their children would look at the exciting posters and immediately want to go to Tom Sawyer Island or elsewhere in the Park."

LEFT Walt in front of attraction posters at the entrance to Disneyland Park, 1956

OPPOSITE LEFT Bjørn Aronsen, *Peter Pan's Flight* attraction poster, 1955; printed ink on paper

OPPOSITE RIGHT Bjørn Aronsen, *Rocket to the Moon* attraction poster, 1955; printed ink on paper

MAIN STREET, U.S.A.

ELEVATION MODELS

CREATED IN 1954 BY JAMES TROUT, these miniature models of Main Street, U.S.A. were used to bring to life the blueprint drawings of the elevations for each building. Before guests could walk down Main Street, these models helped Imagineers envision how Walt's dream of a turn-of-the-century boulevard would come to life. These hand-painted models are made from balsa wood and have incredible detail adorning each one. The windows have a glare to them, and each brick has been hand drawn.

A model of Main Street Station was developed as a concept that was never built for Disneyland. However, the design of a station was instead incorporated into Magic Kingdom Park at Walt Disney World Resort in 1971.

Explained Walt, "It's not apparent at a casual glance, but [Main Street, U.S.A.] is only a scale model. We had every brick and shingle and gas lamp made five-eighths true size. This cost more, but it made the street a toy, and the imagination can play more freely with a toy. Besides, people like to think that their world is somehow more grown-up than Papa's was."

BELOW James F. Trout, Main Street, U.S.A. model segment, c. 1954; balsa wood and acrylic paint

OPPOSITE Green transparent faux kerosene lamp; glass and metal

DISNEYLAND
APARTMENT LAMP

THE INTERIOR OF Walt's Disneyland apartment was decorated in Victorian-era furnishings. In the window that looked out onto Main Street, U.S.A. was this green faux kerosene lamp. As Main Street, U.S.A. transitions in time from the Train Station to the Central Plaza hub, this flickering faux kerosene lamp helps to set the Fire Station firmly within Town Square's turn-of-the-century story. Disneyland Cast Members would often interpret a lit lamp to indicate that Walt was in the apartment when they saw it illuminating the window.

In the early 1980s, Walt's family reclaimed the original furniture and most of the decorations that furnished the apartment, including this lamp—these items now reside in the museum collection, with a selection on view. Though the apartment was later renovated with similar furnishings, today visitors see the window glow with a lamp that stays permanently lit to represent Walt's reassuring presence in Disneyland.

ANIMAL
AUTOMATON TOYS

"It's just animation with sound, run by electronics. AUDIO-ANIMATRONICS. It's an extension of animated drawings. We take an inanimate object and make it move."

—WALT

THESE ORDINARY, UNASSUMING TOYS are evidence of Walt's appreciation of animation in all its forms. In the summer of 1949, Walt took his wife Lillian and daughters Diane and Sharon on vacation to Europe. The family visited England—stopping by the set of *Treasure Island* (1950), Disney's first all-live-action feature—Ireland, Switzerland, and France. One afternoon in Paris, Walt ventured out on his own and did some shopping.

Le Zoo Mechanique, mechanical cat, polar bear, and rabbit, 1949; fur, plastic, metal, and glass

He returned to the hotel room with two large bags filled with a variety of wind-up toys. Diane remembered that moment saying, "He unpackaged them, wound them all up and studied them as we looked on, amused, but puzzled. Not terribly unique, but possibly the forerunners of AUDIO-ANIMATRONICS® figures." Her father saw something in those toys. "It's amazing that you can get such interesting movement from a very simple mechanism," Walt observed.

PIRATES OF THE CARIBBEAN ATTRACTION
STORY SKETCH

THE *PIRATES OF THE CARIBBEAN* ATTRACTION at Disneyland was initially conceived as a walk-through. Imagineer and concept artist Bruce Bushman created drawings for the different scenes that might fit in this model including: "Mary Read's duel to save her lover," shown here.

The idea of a pirate-themed walk-through—a wax museum of sorts—was soon shelved. As Imagineer and scriptwriter Marty Sklar explained, a walk-through story "can be fractured—some people see one thing and miss another, while others can have a different experience."

While the idea of a pirate-orientated attraction remained appealing, it became clear that a walk-through would make it difficult to tell a sequenced story that all Guests could understand. But inspiration struck thanks to the overwhelming success and popularity of *"it's a small world"* at the 1964–1965 New York World's Fair. It was decided a water-based dark ride would house the Imagineers' swashbuckling new creation. The team started to move from idea to sketch, then to sculpture, and finally to full-size AUDIO-ANIMATRONICS® figures.

Pirates of the Caribbean would be the last major attraction Walt developed during his lifetime. In 1965, he walked television audiences on a tour of the attraction via a recreation of the model shop from WED Enterprises—known today as Walt Disney Imagineering. On March 18, 1967, just three and a half months after Walt's passing, *Pirates of the Caribbean* opened to the public at Disneyland. The atmosphere, music, and rich Disney history of the attraction has helped it remain one of the most loved and cherished pieces of Imagineering innovation.

ABOVE Bruce Bushman, concept art for "Mary Read's duel to save her lover", 1957; charcoal and graphite on paper

OPPOSITE TOP Walt with the model for the *Mark Twain Riverboat* attraction, 1955

OPPOSITE BOTTOM *Mark Twain Riverboat* attraction model, c. 1953; wood

MARK TWAIN

RIVERBOAT ATTRACTION MODEL

THE *MARK TWAIN RIVERBOAT* was an opening-day attraction in Frontierland. The Disneyland Publicity Department originally touted it as the first paddle wheeler built in the United States in fifty years. Walt recalled, "One of the biggest joys of my life is sitting on the levee in the Frontierland. ... As I gaze to the north, I can see the smokestacks of the steamer, *Mark Twain*, belching smoke and skirting along toward the tip of Tom Sawyer Island."

Walt was passionate about having the *Mark Twain* at Disneyland. When corporate funding fell short of building the stern-wheeler, Walt helped to finance the construction personally. Walt shared in an article "Frontierland" that was published in *True West* in 1958, "As you can expect from a Missouri-bred boy, I wanted the *Mark Twain* to be authentic. Our staff did extensive research on river boats of the past before [they] came up with a design. Like most of Disneyland, the boat is under-scale to give a fantasy-like appearance. That meant the engines had to be specially built to fit into a smaller craft."

Walt invited Hollywood star Irene Dunne, star of *Showboat* (1936), to christen the maiden voyage of the *Mark Twain Riverboat* on July 17, 1955.

WALLY BOAG'S

CARPET BAG

DISNEYLAND ENTERTAINER Wally Boag opened the Golden Horseshoe Revue in July 1955 as Pecos Bill, where he would aim squirt guns at the audience, spit out a mouthful of "teeth" (lima beans), and sculpt whimsical balloon animals. With a short break in 1971 to open a similar show for the Diamond Horseshoe in the Magic Kingdom Park at Walt Disney World Resort, he would continue his indelible performance three times a day, five times a week, for almost twenty-seven years before retiring in 1982. At the time of his retirement, the *Guinness Book of World Records* listed the show as the longest running stage production in show business history.

Diane Disney Miller remembered, "I first 'met' Wally at my parents' glorious thirtieth anniversary party, July 13, 1955, when he strode on stage at the Golden Horseshoe Saloon with his carpet bag full of gags. It was love at first sight. Like millions of others, including my dad, I never tired of his routine because he was always fresh.

"Dad loved that show. He took all of his guests there, kings and presidents. ... It never got stale.. As a boy in Kansas City, Dad had haunted the vaudeville houses with his pal, Walt Pfeiffer. They sought any opportunity to get on stage and perform their skits. Wally was pure vaudeville, and that's why Dad loved him and the show."

In 2011, Laurence Boag, Wally's son, donated to the museum one of his father's "bag of tricks" that was used for his traveling salesman act. The carpet bag was filled with various props, such as "Boagaloons," which would have been made into various whimsical animals, a bouquet of magically appearing flowers, a skunk prop, and what seemed like an endless supply of broken "teeth."

BELOW Wally Boag's carpet bag used from 1955 to 1982; fabric, leather, and metal

OPPOSITE Wally Boag holding his carpet bag, 1955

ABOVE LEFT Walt in front of World's Fair posters in *Disneyland Goes to the World's Fair* (1964)

ABOVE RIGHT Bob Peak, New York World's Fair 1964–1965 poster, 1961; ink on paper

OPPOSITE TOP Walt and Mary Blair with *"it's a small world"* model, c. 1964

OPPOSITE BOTTOM Mary Blair, abstract sculpture of façade design of *"it's a small world,"* c. 1964; plaster, pigment, mica, glass, iron, fiber, and paper

1964–1965 NEW YORK WORLD'S FAIR
POSTER

THE 1964–1965 NEW YORK WORLD'S FAIR represented a growth point for Walt in many ways. Far more than an opportunity to receive corporate sponsorships that he could utilize in developing new attraction technology, the Fair symbolized the pinnacle of Walt's shared values of futurism and global cooperation. At the same time, the Fair was an opportunity for Walt to test the interest and viability of expanding the Disney theme park experience to the East Coast. Walt was approached about contributing various attractions, which he saw as a great opportunity. He agreed to create four attractions—all of which would end up among the most popular at the Fair—and he gained more than just experience through this endeavor. The State of Illinois' "Great Moments with Mr. Lincoln," "*it's a small world*," the "Primeval World Diorama" (part of the "Magic Skyway" attraction), and the "Carousel of Progress" all eventually relocated to Disneyland.

The successful "test" at the Fair for an East Coast market set the stage for the development of what we know today as Walt Disney World Resort. The idea of a permanent World's Fair showcase of culture and innovation was itself taken as inspiration for the realization of Walt's Experimental Prototype Community of Tomorrow project, known by the acronym EPCOT.

MARY BLAIR

"IT'S A SMALL WORLD" CONCEPT MODEL

IN 1940, MARY BLAIR JOINED The Walt Disney Studios to work on segments for *Fantasia* (1940). The following year, she joined the Disney expedition that toured Mexico and South America. She painted watercolors that inspired Walt to name her as an art supervisor on *Saludos Amigos* (1943) and *The Three Caballeros* (1945). Blair contributed to Disney animated films throughout the 1950s with her imaginative color styling.

In 1964, Walt asked Blair to assist in the design of the overall look and feel of "*it's a small world*" for the 1964–1965 New York World's Fair. "It was the single biggest project that was ever given to her and she was able to just go nuts," marveled her friend and colleague Rolly Crump. For Walt, who never gave up on anything, "it was the climax," noted Ben Sharpsteen, Disney director and producer, of "all the years that [he] spent trying to bring Mary Blair's influence into his productions."

This abstract façade was made with a combination of techniques and materials. It was constructed of cast plaster with mosaic-like design elements, giving us an insight into the many processes that Blair used in her artwork. Some areas are carved out from the plaster background and reinforced with a fibrous component; other sections have an internal wire support with the plaster cast on top; and still others appear to have been constructed with walls and supports that were removed once the plaster was cured.

MARC DAVIS "*IT'S A SMALL WORLD*" CONCEPT SKETCH

MARC DAVIS STARTED AT THE DISNEY STUDIOS as an apprentice animator. During Davis's animation career, he was assigned to and executed some of the most difficult animation for Walt Disney's leading ladies and femmes fatales such as *Peter Pan*'s Tinker Bell, *Sleeping Beauty*'s title heroine Princess Aurora, its villain Maleficent, and *One Hundred and One Dalmatians*' Cruella De Vil. It was Davis's mastery of the human form and authority on anatomy and movement that brought these iconic characters to life and made them believable.

Davis was later asked to help in the planning of attractions at Disneyland and for the 1964–1965 New York World's Fair. His creative contributions include attractions such as *Pirates of the Caribbean*, "*it's a small world,*" and the *Haunted Mansion*, to name a few.

Davis worked with a team of Disney artists and engineers to design the AUDIO-ANIMATRONICS® figures for "*it's a small world,*" including fellow famed artist Mary Blair. Davis was assigned to create concepts and cut-out models for different scenes in the attraction.

ABOVE LEFT Marc Davis, sketch for *"it's a small world,"* c. 1964; ink on paper

BELOW RIGHT Marc and Alice Davis at Tivoli Gardens, c. 1958

OPPOSITE Alice Davis, costume concept drawing for *"it's a small world,"* 1963; photostat on paper

ALICE DAVIS "*IT'S A SMALL WORLD*"
COSTUME DESIGN

ALICE ESTES'S REPUTATION AS A FASHION DESIGNER preceded her. One day, to her surprise, she received a call from her former animation instructor, Marc Davis, at the Disney studio asking her to design a dress for the live-action model of Princess Aurora for then in production animated feature *Sleeping Beauty* (1959). Tom Staggs, former chairman of Walt Disney Parks and Resorts, spoke on the spark between the two artists during the production of *Sleeping Beauty*: "That [*Sleeping Beauty*] costume was exactly what [Marc] was looking for–and so was Alice." The two artists married in 1956.

Years later, Alice Davis got another very important phone call from Marc. "Alice, Walt wants to know if you'd like to do the costumes for '*small world*.'" She leapt at the chance to work with a favorite artist of hers, Mary Blair.

Alice shared, "I designed all of the costumes and the patterns and the choice of fabrics and so on. I was working with Mary Blair, and she was setting the colors that she wanted to go with the sets, and [worked] with Marc for what he wanted the overall look to be. ... And then Walt, of course, would come and give his final approval on everything."

To date, they are the only married couple to have Disneyland Main Street, U.S.A. windows dedicated to them for their contributions to the park.

EPCOT

WALT'S

DREAM FOR EPCOT

AS PART OF HIS AMBITIOUS "FLORIDA PROJECT," Walt Disney envisioned a community space he called "EPCOT," an Experimental Prototype Community of Tomorrow. Later in his life, Walt had become interested in the problems of contemporary city planning and sought to envision a new type of community. His novel approach was to build a place where people could live and work in a dynamic, constantly innovative environment.

Walt said, "We know what our goals are; we know what we hope to accomplish. And believe me, it's the most exciting and challenging assignment we've ever tackled at Walt Disney Productions ... EPCOT will take its cue from the new ideas and new technologies that are now emerging from the creative centers of American industry. It will be a community of tomorrow that will never be completed, but will always be introducing and testing and demonstrating new materials and new systems. And EPCOT will always be a showcase to the world for the ingenuity and imagination of American free enterprise."

Walt's untimely death on December 15, 1966, largely marked the end of the intended creative vision for his Experimental Prototype Community of Tomorrow. However, many of his philosophies were embedded into the later-realized theme park of a similar name, EPCOT Center, which opened on October 1, 1982, at Walt Disney World Resort.

By highlighting host countries from around the globe in World Showcase and innovative new technological ideas in Future World, Walt's concepts for a permanent world's fair celebrating the best of humanity's achievements would indeed live on long past his lifetime.

"But the most exciting, by far the most important part of our Florida project will be our experimental prototype city of tomorrow. We call it EPCOT."

—WALT

OPPOSITE Walt with EPCOT map, 1966

WALT'S

EARLY CONCEPT DRAWING FOR EPCOT

THIS PAPER NAPKIN FEATURES a rough early concept designs for Walt's vision of EPCOT, said to be drawn by Walt, sketched out in blue ink with many arrows, pathways, and round forms. Inscriptions from left to right read: "Covered Mall," "Trucks," "High Rise Business Bldg," "Green Belt Playground Schools Churches," and "Outer Auto Road." Stained, creased, and torn, this sketch was meant to be a temporary way to record Walt's thoughts. According to oral history, this piece was purchased from the son of one of Walt's gardeners, who picked up the napkin and asked to keep it after witnessing Walt drawing and then discarding it.

During the development of his vision for EPCOT, Walt said, "Everything in EPCOT will be dedicated to the happiness of the people who will live, work, and play here ... and those who come here from all around the world to visit our living showcase. We don't presume to know all the answers. In fact, we're counting on the cooperation of American industry to provide their very best thinking during the planning and the creation of our Experimental Prototype Community of Tomorrow. And most important of all, when EPCOT has become a reality and we find the need for technologies that don't even exist today, it's our hope that EPCOT will stimulate American industry to develop new solutions that will meet the needs of people expressed right here in this experimental community."

RIGHT Concept drawing for EPCOT on napkin drawn by Walt, c. 1966; ink on paper

OPPOSITE Sketch of EPCOT transportation drawn by Walt, September 27, 1966; graphite on board

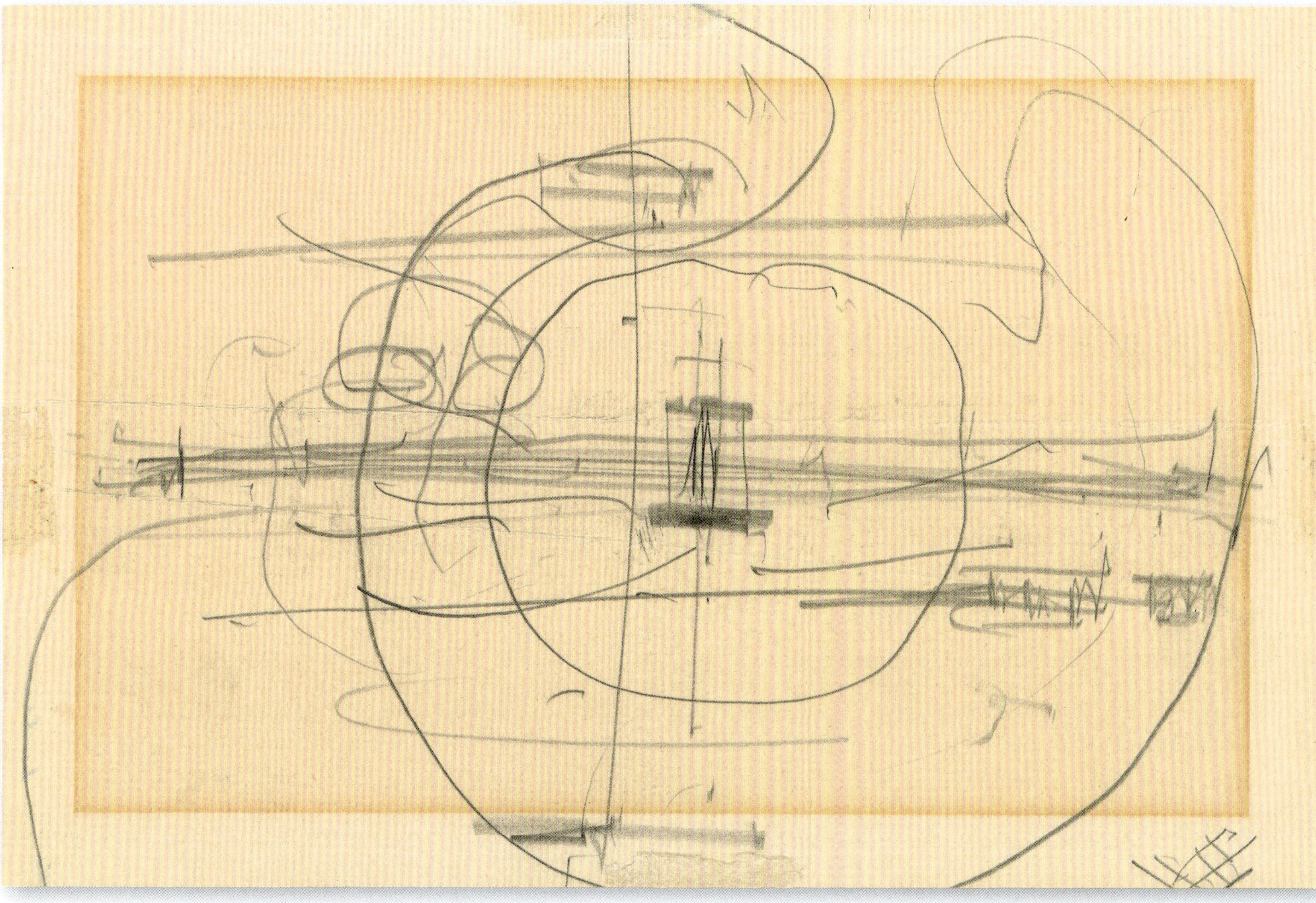

WALT'S

EPCOT TRANSPORTATION SYSTEM DRAWING

FOR EPCOT, WALT SKETCHED OUT IDEAS on how to innovate the transportation system. On September 27, 1966, Walt created these drawings in a meeting on his vision for the interconnected system of public transportation, personal cars, and supply vehicles that would travel throughout the city.

This sketch was picked up after a meeting by the secretary to Imagineer Marvin Davis, Valerie Watson Curry. "While cleaning the room, a sketch on one pad caught [my] eye and [I] asked about it," Curry recalled. "It was Walt's sketch of the EPCOT transportation system he envisioned and had shown attendees at the meeting. Instead of throwing it away, [I] asked for Marvin Davis's permission to keep it, which was granted."

Walt continued to plan his "Disney World" project, even as he lay in his hospital bed. "On the day before he died," Walt's older brother Roy O. Disney said, "Walt lay on the hospital bed staring at the ceiling. It was squares of perforated acoustical tile, and Walt pictured them as a grid map for Disney World. Every four tiles represented a square mile, and he said, 'Now there is where the highway will run. There is the route for the monorail.' He drove himself right up to the end."

PART 8
LEGACY

The day after Walt's passing in 1966, *The New York Times* published an extensive obituary, hailing Walt as "a weaver of fantasies" and taking readers on a journey through his life in all its trials and triumphs. "One day, when Mr. Disney was approaching 60 and his black hair and neatly trimmed mustache were gray, he was asked to reduce his success to a formula. His brown eyes became alternately intense and dreamy ... Maybe it's because I can still be amazed at the wonders of the world.'"

In 1966, with varied projects—EPCOT, a proposed ski resort in Northern California, *The Jungle Book* (1967) in production, and co-founding California Institute of the Arts—Walt hadn't come close to slowing down. As historians Katherine and Richard Greene write, "One of the most remarkable aspects of Walt's final years was the hectic pace of his workday. Entering his 60s and approaching an age when many begin thinking of retirement, Walt worked as if he were just getting started." He never slowed down and never considered stepping back, for there were always more stories to tell and more good work to be done.

BLAINE GIBSON

BUST OF WALT

BLAINE GIBSON BEGAN WORKING at The Walt Disney Studios in 1939. In the 1950s, Walt Disney recognized Gibson's talent for sculping and assigned him to the Disneyland project. In this role, Gibson created hundreds of sculptures, many of which were later used to help develop and produce AUDIO-ANIMATRONICS® figures for Disney theme parks and the 1964–1965 New York World's Fair. He also created this iconic bust of Walt. Gibson's son Wes explained, "With this one-of-a-kind casting, [my dad] was able to capture Walt's appearance when he walked through Walt Disney Imagineering to look at the projects for the World's Fair and Disneyland. This early study of Walt served as a reference point for the creation of the *Partners* statue." The now-iconic Disneyland statue depicts Walt holding the hand of one of his most famous characters, Mickey Mouse. The statue is now featured at four additional Disney locations around the globe.

DR. ADRIAN E. FLATT

CASTS OF WALT'S HANDS

IN THE 1960S, world-renowned orthopedic surgeon Dr. Adrian Flatt began making casts of famous people's hands. Through his unique art form, he wanted to demonstrate that there was not a "typical" type of hand, and that a person's hand shape would not necessarily dictate his or her success in a certain field.

Dr. Flatt collected castings from all kinds of successful people, including artist Norman Rockwell, President Ronald Reagan, professional athletes Wilt Chamberlain and André the Giant, actress Katharine Hepburn, and Walt Disney. Copies of Walt's casts can also be found at the Walt Disney Archives and—with more than 100 pairs of other notable hand casts—at Baylor University Medical Center in Dallas, Texas, as part of the Adrian E. Flatt, M.D., Hand Collection.

Adorning Walt's hands are two rings that he wore regularly. On his left hand is the DeMolay Legion of Honor ring that he was given in the mid-1930s. On his right hand is his Claddagh ring showcasing his proud Irish heritage. While visiting Ireland in 1949, Walt and his wife Lillian purchased matching pairs of Claddagh rings. Walt proudly wore this ring on his right hand and the DeMolay Legion of Honor ring on his left hand for the remainder of his life. Looking at these bronzed hands, Walt wore his Claddagh ring in the traditional way, with the heart facing inward, representing that he was married.

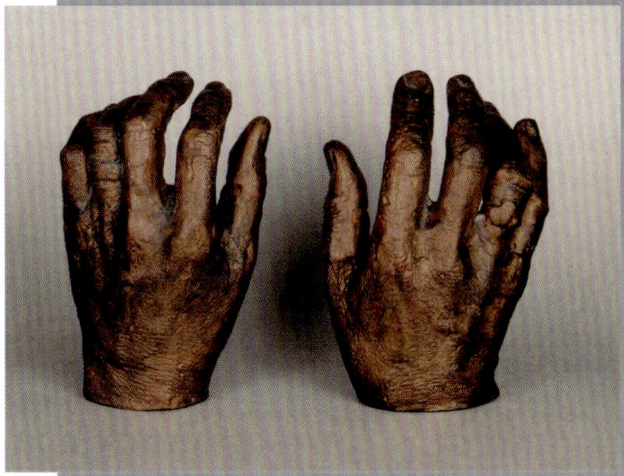

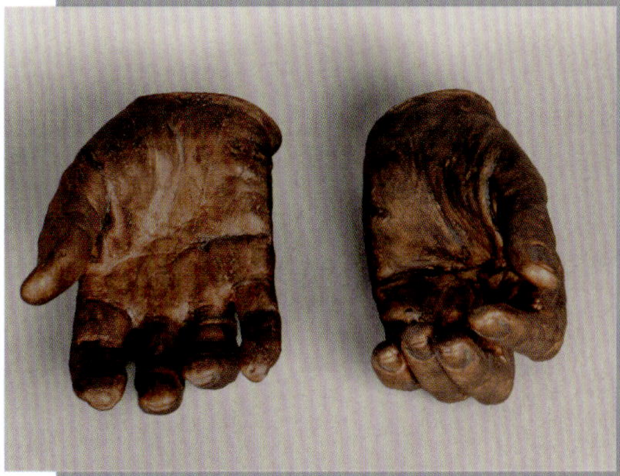

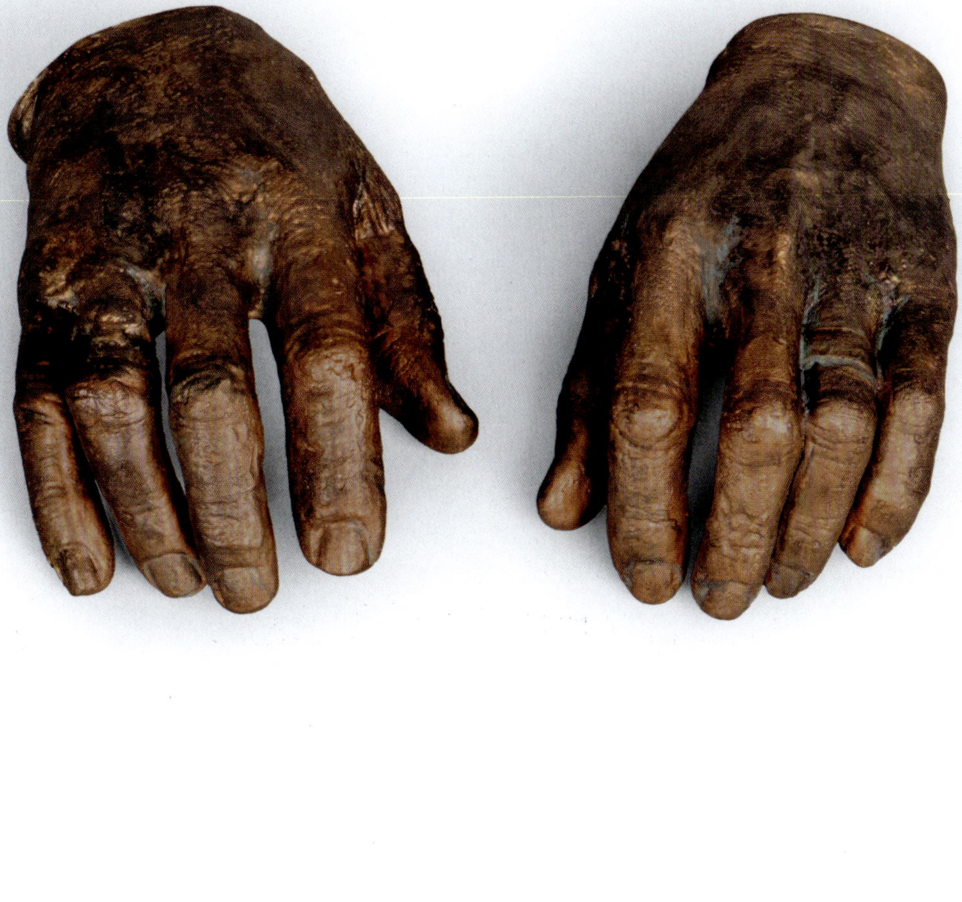

LEFT Adrian E. Flatt, cast of Walt's hands, 1964; paint on plaster

OPPOSITE Blaine Gibson, bust of Walt, 1965; bronze

"On the talents of such citizens rests the future of our American civilization, for it is from the genius of the few that we enrich the greatness of the many."

—PRESIDENT LYNDON B. JOHNSON

WALT'S

PRESIDENTIAL MEDAL OF FREEDOM

THE PRESIDENTIAL MEDAL OF FREEDOM is the nation's highest civilian honor. It is presented to individuals who have made exemplary contributions to the prosperity, values, or security of the United States, world peace, or other significant societal, public, or private endeavors.

In September 1964, Walt Disney was presented with the Presidential Medal of Freedom by President Lyndon B. Johnson at a ceremony in the East Room of the White House. Walt was awarded this honor for his role as "artist and impresario, in the course of entertaining an age, he has created an American folklore."

Walt was one of thirty recipients in 1964 to receive this high distinction. At the ceremony, *The New York Times* reported that President Johnson said of the group's achievements, "[They] have made freedom stronger for all [of] us." The award class of 1964 ranges from Nobel Prize-winning author John Steinbeck to disability rights activist Helen Keller, abstract expressionist painter Willem de Kooning, and Pulitzer Prize–winning poet and biographer Carl Sandburg.

President Johnson ended the ceremony saying, "Our glory is peace, not war; our greatness is in people, not power. The history of America is a history of outstanding achievement by individuals. ... On the talents of such citizens rests the future of our American civilization, for it is from the genius of the few that we enrich the greatness of the many."

RIGHT Presidential Medal of Freedom, 1964; enamel on metal and ribbon

OPPOSITE TOP Walt holding his four Academy Awards, 1954

OPPOSITE BOTTOM Academy Award for Short Subjects, Cartoon, 1969: *Winnie the Pooh and the Blustery Day* (1968); cast metal on plaster

WALT'S

ACADEMY AWARD® COLLECTION

EVEN DECADES AFTER HIS PASSING, Walt Disney still retains the honor of having the most personal Academy Award nominations and the most individual wins.

Walt's Academy Award collection began in 1932, when he took home an Academy Award certificate for the cartoon short *Flowers and Trees* (1932). Walt was also awarded a special Oscar® in 1932 for the creation of Mickey Mouse. At the Academy Award banquet, Walt Disney's humorous short *Parade of the Award Nominees* (1932) was also shown, which depicted whimsical caricatures of that year's Oscar-nominated actors. It was also the first animated appearance of Mickey Mouse produced in color.

From 1932 to 1939, Walt continued to add Academy Awards to his collection by winning for best cartoon short subject each year. At the 1934 ceremony, Walt received an Oscar for the animated short *Three Little Pigs* (1933), which won more than 80 percent of the Academy votes for the honor.

Walt came up to the podium with his head covered in bandages, because he had been injured in a polo match with Will Rogers—the ceremony emcee that same night. Walt shared he was excited to take home his little "Oscar," screenwriter Frances Marion recalled. "Those who had never won the gold-plated honor referred to it disparagingly as the 'Oscar.' But when Walt referred to the 'Oscar' in his speech, that name took on a different meaning, now that we had heard it spoken with sincere appreciation."

ACADEMY OF MOTION PICTURE ARTS AND SCIENCES

IRVING G. THALBERG MEMORIAL AWARD

THE IRVING G. THALBERG MEMORIAL AWARD, named after the legendary vice president and head of production at MGM, is awarded periodically to "creative producers, whose bodies of work reflect a consistently high quality of motion picture production." At the 14th Academy Awards® in 1942, Walt Disney became the youngest honoree at the time and only the fourth recipient of the prestigious honor.

Preceding the Academy giving Walt this honor, the Disney studio had been through a tough year. Walt's most recent animated films *Pinocchio* (1940) and *Fantasia* (1940) did not recoup their initial costs due to World War II blocking the films from being released to European markets. After the bombing of Pearl Harbor in 1941, the Army had moved on to The Walt Disney Studios lot and an estimated 90 percent of all of the studio output would be redirected in support of the American war effort. Accepting the award, Walt said, "I'm well aware of the high ideals that this award symbolizes, and I sort of feel like I should rededicate myself to those ideals. I've been through a very trying year. ... I hope there's never another one like it. And coming after that year, I'd like to feel that it's more than an award for past conscientious efforts, honest mistakes. I like to feel that it's sort of a vote of a confidence for the future."

The Academy felt that his contribution to motion pictures was not only significant, but worthy of one of its highest recognitions. Walt's body of work in 1942, would only be a fraction of what he would achieve in filmmaking in the next twenty-four years of his career.

Shortly after Walt received the award, Thalberg's widow disapproved of the rendering of her husband's bust on the trophy and commissioned a new sculpture. She had the new version of the award, pictured here, sent to Walt and all previous winners.

OPPOSITE Walt holding his Thalberg Award, 1942

LEFT Academy of Motion Pictures, Irving G. Thalberg Memorial Award, 1942; cast metal on wood

MARY BLAIR

MURAL CONCEPT TILE SAMPLE

AN OPHTHALMOLOGIST AND ENTERTAINMENT STUDIO EXECUTIVE, Jules Stein was a lifelong friend and business partner of Walt's who was instrumental in helping him arrange the television deal with ABC to air the *Disneyland* series. In turn, Walt became a loyal supporter of Stein's philanthropic efforts.

Established in 1966, the Jules Stein Eye Institute is a world-renowned center dedicated to the preservation of vision and the prevention of blindness. The Institute's comprehensive programs for the care of patients with eye disorders, research in the vision sciences, education in the field of ophthalmology, and outreach to the community, coupled with its state-of-the-art facilities, have brought national and international recognition to the Institute and UCLA. Walt decided that a simple monetary contribution would be neither a sufficient gift, nor a reflection of his personal friendship with Stein. Instead, Walt commissioned Mary Blair to create a one-of-a-kind ceramic mural for the walls of the Pediatric Waiting Room of the new institute.

Pictured here is Blair's concept rendering and a tile sample for the mural. Blair, working alongside CalArts students and other professionals, worked tirelessly to get the final ceramic mural just right in color and clarity.

BELOW Walt with Doris and Jules Stein holding mural concept, c. 1966

OPPOSITE Mary Blair, ceramic mural of man on elephant for *"it's a small world"* mural for the Jules Stein Eye Institute, 1966; glaze on ceramic

MARINE TOYS FOR TOTS FOUNDATION
AWARD OF APPRECIATION

SHORTLY AFTER TOYS FOR TOTS' INCEPTION IN 1947, The Walt Disney Company began its support. Serving less fortunate children across the nation, Toys for Tots has helped millions of children and teens by providing toys during the holidays. In 1948, Walt and his studio artists designed the famous train logo that is still in use today.

Beyond his creative contributions, Walt was a personal supporter of the Toys for Tots program. He would regularly donate toys and make financial contributions to the program to help ensure its success. Disneyland became a drop-off location for guests to make donations.

Walt's involvement with Toys for Tots helped raise awareness of the program. In 1966, he was presented this award from the U.S. Marine Corps, which runs the charity, as an appreciation for his work with Toys for Tots. Today, the program is still going strong and has helped hundreds of millions of children around the world experience the joy of the holiday season.

SCREEN PRODUCERS GUILD
MILESTONE AWARD

WALT RECEIVED the Screen Producers Guild's Milestone Award on February 17, 1957, at the Grand Ballroom of the Beverly Hills Hilton Hotel. The award is presented annually to a producer who has made "an historic contribution to the entertainment industry."

During the ceremony, Samuel Engel, the president of the Screen Producers Guild, read a message to Walt from President Eisenhower lauding Walt for "[your] contribution to the pleasure and understanding of the world community and your genius as a creator of folklore has long been recognized by leaders in every field of human endeavor, including that most discerning body of critics, the children of this land and all lands. As an artist, your work has helped reveal our country to the world, and the world to all of us. As a man, your sympathetic attitude toward life has helped our children develop a clean and cheerful view of humanity, with all its frailties and possibilities for good."

Cecil B. DeMille, the previous year's recipient, made a tape recording referring to Walt as "Hollywood's poet of celluloid, the man who has brought more sheer joy and happiness to more children of all ages than any other single storyteller who has ever lived."

TOP The Screen Producers Guild Milestone dinner program; printed ink on paper

BOTTOM The Screen Producers Guild Wreath of Honor Milestone Award, 1957; metal on suede mount

OPPOSITE TOP Walt's promotion of Toys for Tots campaign, 1966

OPPOSITE BOTTOM U.S. Marine Corps Award of Appreciation for Toys for Tots, 1966; metal and wood

BOY SCOUTS OF AMERICA

SILVER BUFFALO AWARD MEDAL

"Every kid ... wants and needs to belong to some team or club which has his respect, and which gives him a welcome hand."

—WALT

FOUNDED IN 1910, THE BOY SCOUTS OF AMERICA prepares young people to make ethical and moral choices over their lifetimes by instilling in them such values as loyalty, kindness, and bravery. Created in 1925, the Silver Buffalo Award is Scouting's highest commendation and is "bestowed upon those who give truly noteworthy and extraordinary service to youth."

On May 17, 1946, Walt and his wife Lillian traveled to St. Louis, Missouri, for the awards ceremony. Walt's fellow recipients included Arctic explorer Vilhjalmur Stefansson; United Service Organizations (USO) co-founder Frank Well; then-General of the U.S. Army and future president of the United States, Dwight D. Eisenhower; and World War II veteran and admiral Chester William Nimitz. Walt's Silver Buffalo Award was for contributing "to the joy of youth in every land ... and the elevation of their standards of good taste."

Walt joined the Boy Scouts of America in 1914 in Kansas City, Missouri, and shared of his experience, "American Scouting was four years old when I joined a Patrol formed from the Sunday school class of the Congregational Church. ... It was a great event in my young life, even if circumstances were to prevent my going beyond the Tenderfoot rank." In a newspaper interview covering the award ceremony, Walt noted he had not mentioned being a Boy Scout to the selection committee, but that they knew anyway.

RIGHT Boy Scouts of America Silver Buffalo Award, 1946; metal on ribbon

OPPOSITE TOP Walt and Lillian receiving the Key to the City of San Francisco from Mayor George Christopher, December 10, 1958

OPPOSITE BOTTOM Key to the City of San Francisco, 1958; ink on paper mounted on wood

WALT'S

KEY TO THE CITY OF SAN FRANCISCO

WALT WAS NO STRANGER TO THE CITY OF SAN FRANCISCO or the greater Bay Area, visiting the region numerous times throughout his career. Over the years he visited the region to attend such events as the Golden Gate International Exposition of 1939 and the San Francisco premiere of *Fantasia* (1940) at the Geary Theater.

On December 10, 1958, Mayor George Christopher presented Walt and Lillian Disney with the Key to the City of San Francisco. The reception was held at the San Francisco Museum of Art–known today as SFMOMA. President of the board of the San Francisco Museum of Art E. Morris Cox presented Walt with artist Gurdon Woods's abstract sculpture "Seed" in recognition of his contributions to the arts.

One of the unique threads connecting Walt Disney with San Francisco is this Key to the City. The back of the key says "Please Come Again"–an offer that the Disney family took to heart in opening The Walt Disney Family Museum in San Francisco in 2009.

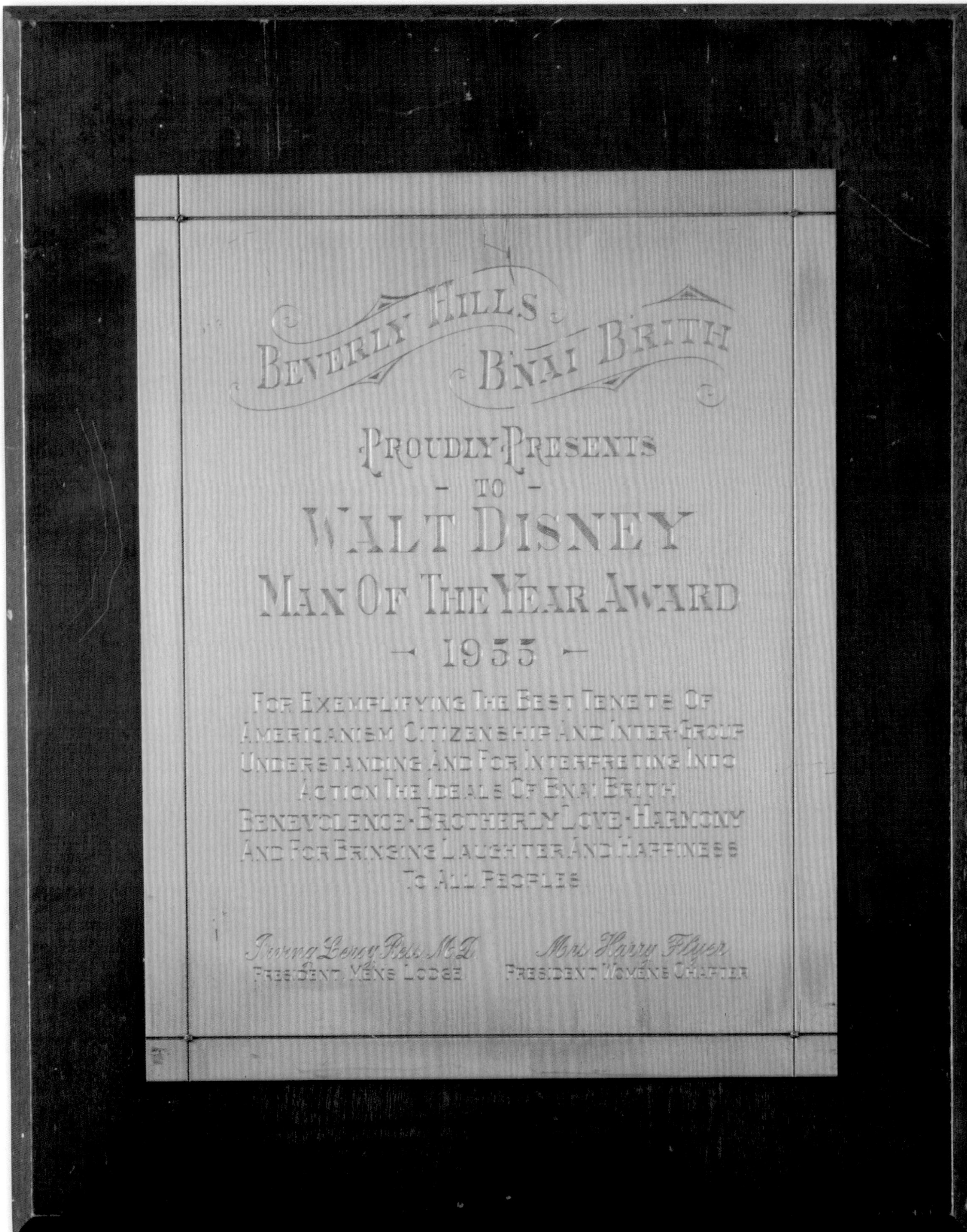

BEVERLY HILLS
B'NAI BRITH
PROUDLY PRESENTS
- TO -
WALT DISNEY
MAN OF THE YEAR AWARD
1955
FOR EXEMPLIFYING THE BEST TENETS OF
AMERICANISM CITIZENSHIP AND INTER-GROUP
UNDERSTANDING AND FOR INTERPRETING INTO
ACTION THE IDEALS OF B'NAI BRITH
BENEVOLENCE · BROTHERLY LOVE · HARMONY
AND FOR BRINGING LAUGHTER AND HAPPINESS
TO ALL PEOPLES
PRESIDENT MEN'S LODGE
PRESIDENT WOMEN'S CHAPTER

BEVERLY HILLS AND KANSAS CITY CHAPTERS

B'NAI B'RITH AWARDS

THE INDEPENDENT ORDER OF B'NAI B'RITH (meaning the "Sons of the Covenant" in Hebrew) is the oldest continually operating Jewish service organization in the world. It was founded in New York City in 1843, and today continues to combat anti-Semitism and Holocaust denial while supporting human rights.

In 1955, Walt was presented with the Beverly Hills B'nai B'rith "Man of the Year" Award for exemplifying the best tenets of Americanism, citizenship, and intergroup understanding and for interpreting into action the ideals of B'nai B'rith benevolence.

A second B'nai B'rith award, given to Walt by the Heart of America chapter in Kansas City in 1958, was a Distinguished Service Citation. This award was in recognition of Walt's outstanding continued service in the field of entertainment for children. The award states, "All of B'nai B'rith's services in America seek to promote understanding, cooperation, goodwill among Americans of every race and creed. We feel our philanthropic worth with children is one of our most important services. We B'nai B'rith women feel that Mr. Disney's intelligent imaginative production for television and movies serve as a challenging force for wholesome, educational entertainment."

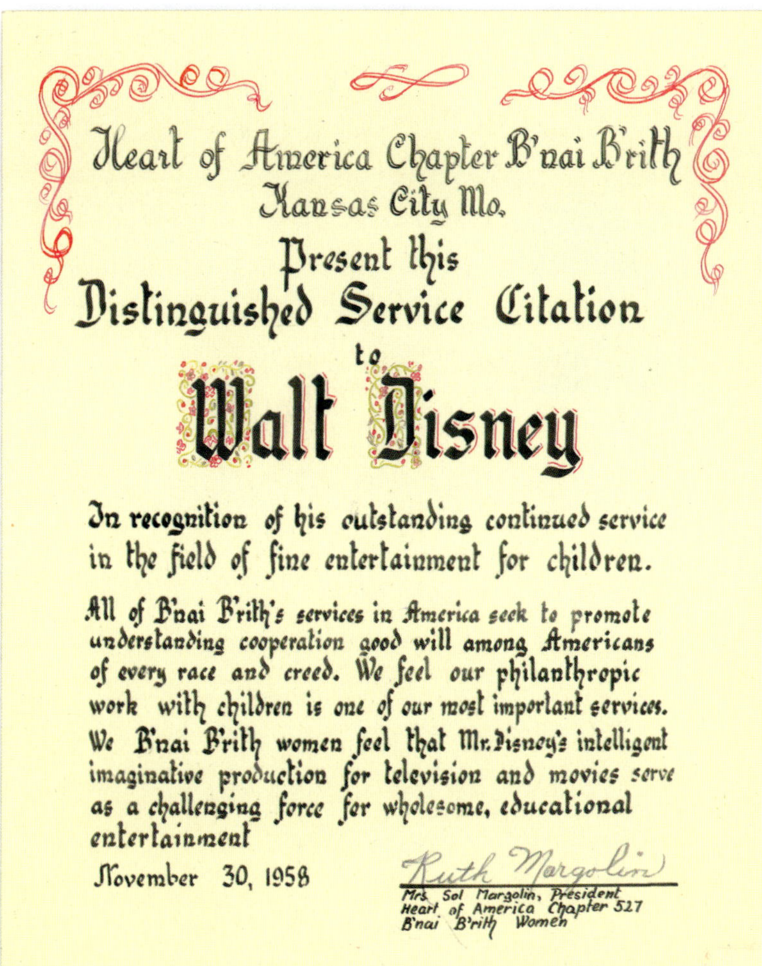
Heart of America Chapter B'nai B'rith
Kansas City Mo.
Present this
Distinguished Service Citation
to
Walt Disney

In recognition of his outstanding continued service in the field of fine entertainment for children.

All of B'nai B'rith's services in America seek to promote understanding cooperation good will among Americans of every race and creed. We feel our philanthropic work with children is one of our most important services. We B'nai B'rith women feel that Mr. Disney's intelligent imaginative production for television and movies serve as a challenging force for wholesome, educational entertainment

November 30, 1958

Ruth Margolin
Mrs. Sol Margolin, President
Heart of America Chapter 527
B'nai B'rith Women

"I learned to believe in the basic principle of the right of man to exercise his faith and thoughts as he chooses."

—WALT

LEFT Kansas City B'nai B'rith Distinguished Service Citation, 1958; handwritten and printed ink on paper

OPPOSITE Beverly Hills B'nai B'rith Man of the Year Award, 1955; engraved metal on wood

GOVERNMENT OF MEXICO

ORDER OF THE AZTEC EAGLE AWARD

ON AUGUST 30, 1943, Walt received the Order of the Aztec Eagle, the highest honor a non-national can receive from the Mexican government. Along with co-founder of MGM Studios, Louis B. Mayer, Walt went to Mexico City to receive their medals directly from Mexican president Manuel Ávila Camacho. The award honored those who have made a great contribution to Mexico, in particular, or humankind in general, and focused on Walt's efforts to foster beneficial international relations with Mexico.

Two years prior, in 1941, Walt had traveled with a hand-selected group of artists through Latin American countries as part of President Roosevelt's Good Neighbor policy. Walt's team met presidents, artists, and common folk alike while developing stories and artwork for animated films based on the culture and landscapes of the nations they visited. Part of the group made their way through Mexico on the return trip home, while others would make return visits in the ensuing years to seek further inspiration for studio projects from the region.

Walt continued to have favorable relations with Mexico throughout his life.

RIGHT Order of the Aztec Eagle from Mexico, 1943; metal and ribbon

OPPOSITE LEFT Walt wearing his DeMolay Legion of Honor ring, 1962

OPPOSITE RIGHT DeMolay Founder's Cross and Legion of Honor ring, 1937; cast metal and ribbon

DEMOLAY INTERNATIONAL

FOUNDER'S CROSS AND RING

DEMOLAY INTERNATIONAL, founded in Kansas City, Missouri, in 1919, is an organization dedicated to preparing young men to lead successful, happy, and productive lives. On May 29, 1920, Walt became a member of the Kansas City Chapter of the foundational incarnation of the group, the Order of DeMolay for boys. Walt shared, "One of the most important events of my youth, and one of the happiest too, was my acceptance into the membership of DeMolay. ... I was among the first members of the order when it was conceived and established in Kansas City, Missouri."

In 1937, Walt traveled to Kansas City, Missouri, to attend the Order of DeMolay conference. Founder Frank S. Land presented the Order of DeMolay Founder's Cross representing his membership and dedication to the Kansas City Chapter. The gold Legion of Honor ring, also from the 1930s, features DeMolay symbols around the band. Walt would regularly wear this ring proudly on his left hand throughout the remainder of his life.

Writing to DeMolay's Acacia Chapter in Stuart, Florida, in 1965, Walt said: "I feel a great sense of obligation and gratitude toward the Order for the part it has played in my endeavors. Its precepts have been beyond value in making decisions, in facing dilemmas and crises, in holding onto faith and ideals, and in meeting the tests which are best borne when shared with others in a bond of confidence and mutual respect."

FRANCE

LEGION OF HONOR AWARD

ESTABLISHED BY NAPOLEON BONAPARTE IN 1802, Ordre Nation de la Legion d'Honneur—the Legion of Honor Award—commends people for their service to France regardless of their social class or rank. The award carries the distinction of being the highest civil or military honor in France. Non-nationals can be awarded the medal for service to France and for their ideals.

Walt volunteered for the American Red Cross during World War I. Although the war had ended by the time he arrived in France, he spent eleven months there driving an ambulance and other service vehicles, and would later consider it as the most transformative time in his life. When Walt would take his family to France decades later, he toured them through the towns and locations where he had served.

On January 8, 1936, French consul general Jean Joseph Viala presented Walt with the Legion of Honor medal at the Disney studio on Hyperion Avenue in Los Angeles. The award was signed by His Excellency the President of the Republic of France, Léon Blum, and recognized Walt for his work shaping the animated art form and spreading goodwill around the world.

THE HOLLYWOOD FOREIGN PRESS ASSOCIATION

CECIL B. DEMILLE AWARD

FOUNDED IN 1943 by a correspondent for the British *Daily Mail* newspaper, the Hollywood Foreign Press Association (HFPA) is comprised of journalists who cover the U.S. film industry but are affiliated with publications outside of North America. Presented annually for motion pictures and television programs, the Golden Globe Awards have been a HFPA fundraiser for philanthropic activities since 1944. One of the most prestigious prizes given out at the awards is the Cecil B. DeMille Award.

The Cecil B. DeMille Award for lifetime achievement in motion pictures was named in honor of Cecil B. DeMille (1881–1959), one of the industry's most successful filmmakers. The HFPA created the award in 1952 to recognize "outstanding contributions to the entertainment field."

On April 2, 1953, Walt wrote to DeMille after receiving the award, "I want to thank you for the tribute you paid us at the Hollywood Foreign Correspondents' Awards Dinner. You were most generous as you always have been in your laudatory remarks about our work. I felt a deep sense of gratitude in receiving the DeMille Award and, then having your daughter, Cecilia, make the presentation, it was indeed an event that touched me."

OPPOSITE TOP French consul general presenting Walt with the French Legion of Honor, January 8, 1936

OPPOSITE BOTTOM Ordre Nation de la Legion d'Honneur, 1936; enamel on metal and ribbon

LEFT Cecil B. DeMille Award from the Hollywood Foreign Press, 1953; cast metal and marble

WALT'S
HONORARY COLLEGE DEGREES

WALT PARTICIPATED IN MANY COMMENCEMENT CEREMONIES, but attended just one year of high school. Walt left his formal education behind in 1918 to serve as an auxiliary chauffeur for the Red Cross in the aftermath of World War I. Instead of learning from behind a desk, Walt pieced together an education through his own life experiences, using the world as his classroom.

Walt's extraordinary accomplishments caught the attention of several prestigious universities, which awarded him honorary degrees.

USC, Harvard, and Yale all commended Walt for his contributions to society. Harvard's president said, "Walt Disney is a magician who has created a modern dwelling for the Muses...." After the Harvard ceremony, Walt told *The American Magazine*, "I'm grateful for these honorary degrees and the distinction they confer. But I'll always wish I'd had the chance to go through college in the regular way and earn a plain Bachelor of Arts like the thousands of kids nobody ever heard of, who are being graduated today."

USC's president spoke of Walt's achievement in "bringing to youngsters the spirit of innocent childhood, and bringing to oldsters a bit of their second childhood." In the case of Yale, Walt's name had been on the list of proposed recipients as early as 1935. Correspondences between administrators and staff said Walt had "done more to endear America to the hearts of foreigners than the entire state department put together, inventing America's ambassador."

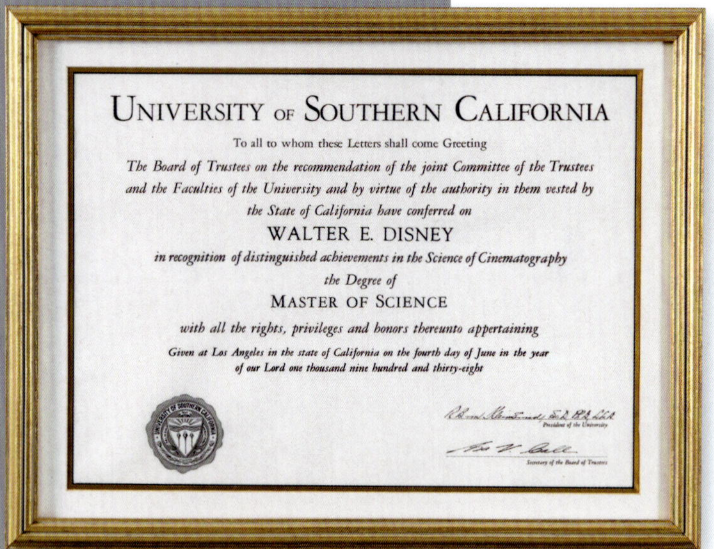

UNIVERSITY OF SOUTHERN CALIFORNIA

To all to whom these Letters shall come Greeting

The Board of Trustees on the recommendation of the joint Committee of the Trustees and the Faculties of the University and by virtue of the authority in them vested by the State of California have conferred on

WALTER E. DISNEY

in recognition of distinguished achievements in the Science of Cinematography

the Degree of

MASTER OF SCIENCE

with all the rights, privileges and honors thereunto appertaining

Given at Los Angeles in the state of California on the fourth day of June in the year of our Lord one thousand nine hundred and thirty-eight

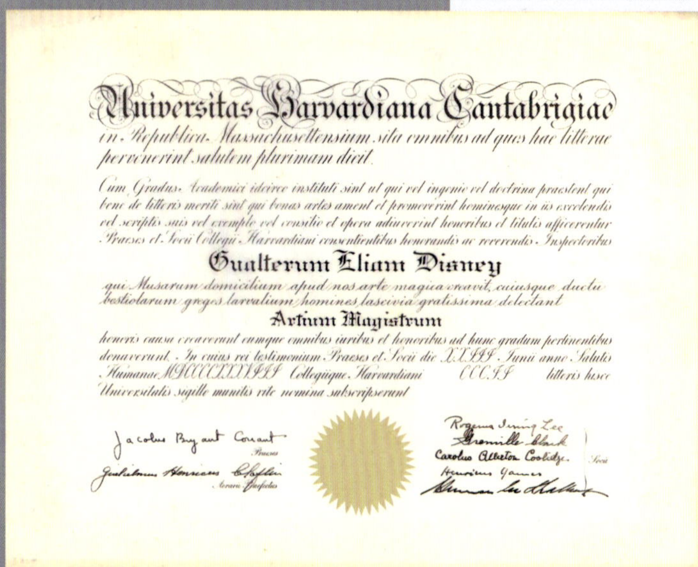

Universitas Harvardiana Cantabrigiae

Gualterum Eliam Disney

Artium Magistrum

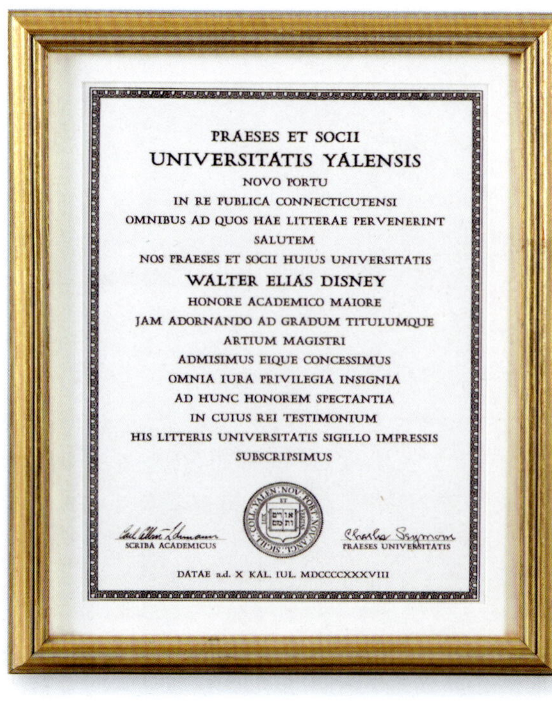

PRAESES ET SOCII
UNIVERSITATIS YALENSIS
NOVO PORTU
IN RE PUBLICA CONNECTICUTENSI
OMNIBUS AD QUOS HAE LITTERAE PERVENERINT
SALUTEM
NOS PRAESES ET SOCII HUIUS UNIVERSITATIS
WALTER ELIAS DISNEY
HONORE ACADEMICO MAIORE
IAM ADORNANDO AD GRADUM TITULUMQUE
ARTIUM MAGISTRI
ADMISIMUS EIQUE CONCESSIMUS
OMNIA IURA PRIVILEGIA INSIGNIA
AD HUNC HONOREM SPECTANTIA
IN CUIUS REI TESTIMONIUM
HIS LITTERIS UNIVERSITATIS SIGILLO IMPRESSIS
SUBSCRIPSIMUS

SCRIBA ACADEMICUS — PRAESES UNIVERSITATIS

DATAE a.d. X KAL. IUL. MDCCCCXXXVIII

FROM TOP Honorary Master of Science Degree from University of Southern California, 1938; handwritten and printed ink on paper; Honorary Master of Arts Degree from Harvard University, 1938; handwritten and printed ink on paper; Honorary Master of Arts Degree from Yale University, 1938; handwritten and printed ink on paper

OPPOSITE Walt in Harvard University cap and gown with character dolls, 1938

NATO
SOPHIA LOREN

NATIONAL ASSOCIATION OF THEATER OWNERS

"SHOWMAN OF THE YEAR" AWARD

ON OCTOBER 1, 1966, the National Association of Theatre Owners bestowed the prestigious Showman of the Year award upon Walt at what would turn out to be his final public appearance before his passing two months later. It was conceived as an annual prize, but due to the grave loss later that year, the association retired the award, making Walt the only showman to be the recipient of this honor. Fittingly, the plaque is inscribed with: "He is, indeed, the first ... perhaps the only ... Showman of the World. He is, of course, Walt Disney."

In his acceptance speech, Walt said, "Before sitting down to count my blessings, I want to make you a promise. I promise we won't let this great honor you have paid us tonight go to our head–we have too many projects for the future to take time out for such a thing. On top of that, after forty-some-odd-years of ups and downs in this crazy business of ours, we know too well–you are only as good as your next picture."

> **"He is, indeed, the first ... perhaps the only ... Showman of the World. He is, of course, Walt Disney."**
>
> —NATIONAL ASSOCIATION OF THEATRE OWNERS

OPPOSITE Walt and Sophia Loren with Showman of the World Award, 1966

LEFT Showman of the World Award, 1966; printed ink on wood

OVERLEAF Walt on the Carolwood Pacific Railroad, c. 1949

173

C.P.R.R.
1212
C.P.R.R.
6666
C.P.R.R.

ACKNOWLEDGMENTS

The Walt Disney Family Museum presents the fascinating story and achievements of Walt Disney, the man who raised animation to the level of fine art, transformed the film industry, tirelessly pursued innovation, and created a global, yet distinctively American legacy. The museum was co-founded by Walt Disney's eldest daughter, Diane Disney Miller, and her son Walter Miller in October 2009. Diane recalled, "Beyond being the risk-taking visionary who created an entertainment empire and left a lasting legacy on American culture, Walt Disney was an actual man, a loving son and brother, a doting husband, a loyal friend and a wonderful father—more importantly my father."

Located in the scenic San Francisco Presidio, The Walt Disney Family Museum features innovative technology alongside a vast collection of historic materials and artifacts that bring Disney's achievements to life. Early drawings and animation, movies, music, listening stations, a spectacular model of Disneyland, and much more are presented in a myriad of interactive galleries. The museum is a 501(c)(3) nonprofit organization.

"Animation, Innovation, Inspiration—you'll find it all here in the story of my father's life, and it may inspire you, too."

—Diane Disney Miller

CREDITS

Photography of objects by Mark Gibson and Michael Grassia; photographs of the portraits on page 103 by Victoria Wall Harris.

All objects belong to the Walt Disney Family Foundation except where noted below.

Artwork and Artifact Lenders: Courtesy of Alice Davis: 198 right; Courtesy of Jennifer Goff: 24 top, 37; Courtesy Michelle Lund: 103; Courtesy of Joanna Miller: 180 top; Courtesy of *The Saturday Evening Post*: 187; Courtesy of Ryan Scheer: 172; Courtesy of the Walt Disney Animation Research Library: 147; Courtesy of the Walt Disney Archives: 64, 65, 73, 151.

Artwork and Artifact Donors: Gift of Dean Barickman: 80 left, 185, 186 right, 192; Mary Blair Collection: 197, 199; Gift of the Boag Family: 194; Gift of the Pam Burns-Clair Family: 198 left; Gift of the California Institute of the Arts: 80 right; Gift of Valerie Watson Curry: 203; Gift of Suzanne Hiller Herrick: 143 left; Gift of Don Hahn: 70; Gift of Don Iwerks: 155; Ollie Johnston Collection: 133; Ward Kimball Collection: 25 top, 116; Gift of Rick Law: 128; Anonymous gift in memory of Diane Disney Miller: 63 middle and bottom, 115; Gift of Diane Disney Miller: 21 right, 22 bottom, 23 left, 32 right, 35, 43 bottom, 61, 63, 97, 127 right, 156 top, 174, 177, 178, 179, 181, 215 top; Gift of Ron and Diane Miller: 13 left, 22 top, 23 right, 38 bottom, 43 top, 44, 89 bottom, 104, 105, 106, 118, 126, 127 middle, 145, 157, 186 left, 202; Gift of Walter E. D. Miller: 7, 12 bottom, 25 bottom, 41, 53 bottom, 58, 88, 95, 142, 143 right, 196 right; Gift of The Walt Disney Company: 18, 34, 81, 175 bottom, 207.

Artwork and Artifact Copyright: all images are © Disney except where noted below.

© Academy of Motion Picture Arts and Sciences: 209 top and bottom, 210; "OSCAR" "IRVING G. THALBERG MEMORIAL AWARD" statuette © A.M.P.A.S.®: 24 top and bottom, 69, 112, 211; San Francisco History Center, San Francisco Public Library: 217, 225; Walt Disney Archives: 12 left, 19, 51 top, 55 top, 59, 91, 196 left; Walt Disney Family Foundation: 21 right, 22 top, 22 bottom, 23 right, 34, 38 top and bottom, 40, 43 top, 44, 45 all, 53 top, 56, 57, 58, 62, 63 all, 64, 65, 66, 68, 70, 71, 74 (Harper Goff Collection), 75 top, 86, 89 all, 90, 94, 95, 96, 98, 99, 100, 101, 104 left and right, 106, 157, 175 bottom, 189, 194, 202, 209 bottom, 222 top, 224 middle.

Photo credits: all photos are courtesy of Walt Disney Archives except where noted below.

Alamy/PictureLux/The Hollywood Archive: 91; Getty Images/Bettman: 221; Getty Images/Bettman Corbis: 33; Getty Images/Tom Nebbia/Corbis: 29.

THE WALT DISNEY COMPANY

Corporate Brand Management
Charlie Cain

Corporate Legal
Margaret Adamic

Disney Publishing Worldwide
Jennifer Eastwood
Hunter Heller
Wendy Lefkon
Angela Grief
Daniel Saeva
Krista Wong

Disney Parks, Experiences and Products Legal
Chrissy Cox

Walt Disney Animation Research Library
Fox Carney
Tori Cranner
Doug Engalla
Jackie Vasquez
Marisa Leonardi

Walt Disney Animation Studios
Amy Astley

Walt Disney Archives
Rebecca Cline
Joanna Pratt
Matthew Adams
Nicole Carroll
Michael Buckhoff
Cesar Gallegos
Jeff Golden
Kevin M. Kern
Ed Ovalle
Ty Popko
Francesca Scrimgeour
Steven Vagnini
Julia Vargas

THE WALT DISNEY FAMILY MUSEUM

The Walt Disney Family Museum Board of Directors
Walter E. D. Miller
Christopher Miller
Tamara Diane Miller
Michelle Lund
Reilly Miller
Haley Scheer
Charlotte Goff
Madeline Goff
Kirsten Komoroske
Pat Gallagher

Walt Disney Family Foundation Board of Directors
Christopher Miller
Joanna Miller
Jennifer Miller Goff

The Walt Disney Family Museum and Walt Disney Family Foundation Staff
Elizabeth Anderson
Christine Baez
Marlon Baez
Maryellen Beauperthuy
Bri Bertolaccini
Maureen Bourbin
Summer Brown
Kaitlin Buickel-Manosca
Miles Burton
Natalie Chan
Maya Colbert
Paige Collins
Elora Cuenco
Aaron Devera
Fiorella Edwards
John Ferris
Roberto Flores
Alyson Fried
Emmeline Geyer
Mark Gibson
Carla Gonzalez
Melaney Gonzalez
Madison Gordon
Bethany Hall
Lara Hayner
Nicole Hellmann
Aimee Hironaka-Juteau
Kyle Hoctor
Julian Jimenez-Montano
Alyssa Joyce
Sarah Kennedy
Zaeem Kitsos
Kirsten Komoroske
Camila Krenn
Jenna L'Italien-Uppal
Travis Lacina
Grace Lacuesta
Katherine Langdon
Daniella Llamas
Cindy Lutz
Marisa Major
Daniel Mendoza
Anita Meza
Caitlin Moneypenny-Johnston
Chris Mullen
Amanda Nguyen
Mayumi Nguyen
Andrew J. Nilsen
Brian O'Hara
William Palomares
Julia Pichay
Caroline Quinn
Steven Reder
Rueben Rodriguez
Martin Salazar
Ivana Santos
Maureen Shields
Senah Keri Simms
Frances Souza
Rick Stone
Peter Susoev
Tracie Timmer
Emily Vann Green
Marina Villar Delgado
Theresa Von Dohlen
Charlotte Weller
Celeste Zambrano

weldon**owen**

an imprint of Insight Editions
P.O. Box 3088
San Rafael, CA 94912
www.weldonowen.com

CEO Raoul Goff
VP Publisher Roger Shaw
Editorial Director Katie Killebrew
Senior Editor Karyn Gerhard
Project Editor Jen Newens
Editorial Assistant Jon Ellis
VP Creative Chrissy Kwasnik
Art Director and Designer Allister Fein
VP Manufacturing Alix Nicholaeff
Senior Production Manager Joshua Smith
Sr Production Manager, Subsidiary Rights Lina s Palma-Temena

The Walt Disney Family Museum
Author, Museum Co-founder, and President of the Board of Directors: Walter E. D. Miller
Content and Research Manager: Bri Bertolaccini

Executive Director: Kirsten Komoroske
Chief of Staff: Alyson Fried
Director of Exhibitions and Collections: Marina Villar Delgado
Director of Marketing and Communications: Caitlin Moneypenny-Johnston
Exhibitions Manager: Kaitlin Buickel-Manosca

Additional text and research by Bri Bertolaccini, Jen Newens, Lucas O. Seastrom, and Caroline Quinn

Editing and fact-checking by Margaret Adamic, Michael Buckhoff, Kaitlin Buickel-Manosca, Miles Burton, Fox Carney, Kevin M. Kern, Caitlin Moneypenny-Johnston, Ed Ovalle, Paula Sigman Lowery, and Theresa Von Dohlen

Weldon Owen would also like to thank Michael Grassia, Jen Newens, Jon Ellis, and Karen Levy for their extraordinary work on this project.

Library of Congress Cataloging in Publication data is available.
ISBN: 978-1-68188-448-6
10 9 8 7 6 5 4 3 2
Printed in China

Published by The Walt Disney Family Foundation Press, LLC.
104 Montgomery Street in the Presidio
San Francisco, CA 94129